OUT OF DARKNESS

OUT OF DARKNESS

Possessed . . . Rescued . . . Forgiven

George Osborn with Becci Brown

Authentic

Out of Darkness
Copyright © George Osborn

Reprinted 2014, 2015 and 2017

23 22 21 20 19 18 17   11 10 9 8 7 6 5 4

First published 2014 by Authentic Media Limited
PO Box 6326, Bletchley, Milton Keynes, MK1 9GG.
www.authenticmedia.co.uk

British Library Cataloguing in Publication Data

A catalogue record for this book is available from the British Library

ISBN 978-1-86024-839-9
978-1-78078-068-9 (e-book)

Cover Design by Trust Media Distribution
Printed and bound by CPI Group (UK) Ltd., Croydon, CR0 4YY

Acknowledgements

I would like to give the utmost thanks to the author of my life, the one who created, redeemed and loved me enough to reach out to me in the pit. I acknowledge the hard work that my wife often has to put into my life, and her amazing patience and encouragement. Becci Brown who did most of the work on this book is a testament to perseverance. I thank my mum and sister for being so understanding and willing. My thanks go to the reader, too, for taking the time to read this story which I feel compelled to tell.

George Osborn
May 2014

Disclaimer

Some names and details have been changed to protect the identity of the individuals concerned. However this is a true story and all other details have been presented as accurately as memory allows at the time of writing.

Contents

Prologue

Scudding across the sky, the clouds seemed carefree. As I lay there, watching them, I wondered if they could see, and what they thought about. The wood I was lying on felt smooth, like a series of slats on a bed, but the sharp pebbles between each slat jabbed at me, insisting I didn't belong there.

'George, get up. Move!'

'Are you mad? What are you doing?'

Above me, halfway to the clouds, I could see my friends on the bridge, terror written across their faces.

We often stood on that bridge, which rose above the tracks that anonymously ferried commuters, day-trippers and holidaymakers, their minds full of other places. For us it was nothing more than a link between the park and a housing estate, small and unconcerned with the elsewhere. Here we'd have a smoke, drink a can of beer and conjure up games of teenage mischief. We'd dare each other to hop over the wire fence, run down the grassy embankment and leap over the railway tracks in front of an oncoming train.

I felt it before they started pointing. Below me the earth rumbled, sending little shivers of vibrating track through my body.

'George! There's a train coming. Get up!' The urgency was tangible in their voices, their fear increasing.

'George, stop being stupid. Move!'

What they didn't realize, as I lay there spread across the track linking Woking to London, was that I had been pinned down. I couldn't get up. I was paralysed.

It would be clichéd and untrue to claim my life flashed before me. But how did a teenage kid with his whole life ahead of him get to this point? Where did it all begin?

It all began with Wellington boots.

Chapter 1

In the Beginning

I shifted from one foot to the other, staring down at my black Wellington boots. The corner felt safe. 'Out there' didn't. Hands in the sand, faces poking through windows in Wendy houses, paint splattered on paper . . . A large, pink hand grabbed mine, enveloping it, hiding it, pulling it.

'Come on, George, let's read a story together.'

I couldn't manage 'together' at 4. So my teacher, Mrs Ross-Waddell read to me about a little monkey looking for a hug. He went to every other animal and they turned him away. Eventually, I remember, he found his mum.

Years later I could be found in this same room, what was once my pre-school, chasing my youth leader with a stick, can of beer in hand. But this was the beginning.

Of course this wasn't *really* where it all began. I came screaming into the world on 5 August 1978 in High Wycombe, Buckinghamshire. We lived in the town of Amersham for the first years of my life, and then moved to Woking when I was 4. Like many, we moved where the work was, and Dad had secured a job with Crown Life, an insurance company; he was tasked with getting their computer systems to work more efficiently.

But this, the pre-school in Woking, was my earliest memory – Wellington boots, new people and a new place.

Walking home from pre-school was like flicking through an ornithologist's journal. In an attempt to bring colourful character to our otherwise modern grey housing estate, each street was endowed with the name of a bird. Swallow Rise, Larks Way, and around the corner to Finch Close. That's where our house stood, in its semi-detached, unremarkable nature – in a quiet street surrounded by other 1970s semis, filled with middle-class people going about their middle-class lives behind closed doors. Only the children would mix and mingle on the streets, a no-man's land dividing territories. There were little boys behind those doors waiting to be my friends, waiting to grow up with me, influence me, get into trouble with me. But for now, having just moved to Woking, there were still boxes stacked in the loft and the little shed, objects of affection yet to find their home. The house was beginning to take shape, the gaps slowly filling in, cluttering up with objects gathered, stored, held onto; the practical and the sentimental. While Mum struggled to remember where she had put things, I enjoyed the adventure of new nooks and crannies, a different view from my window, and toys being pulled from boxes as if they were brand new.

Sometimes, when my pre-school day had ended, Mum and I would meander into Woking rather than going home. The high street bustled with people running errands, heaving packages to the post office, rifling through bargains in the charity shops, selecting cuts of meat at the butcher's, with small children being pushed around in prams and pre-schoolers looking swamped and grubby in uniforms. Mum might pick up a paper or some fish for dinner, but mostly we would head to a small street underneath an archway.

'What do you think, George? Is he going to look?'

I liked this game – waiting under Dad's window at Crown Life, wondering if he'd see us. Before mobile phones there were no texts, just a quiet wait or a wave. Would the flash of colour, of movement, catch his eye? It was fun to stand and watch him scribble, furrow his brows and work things out until eventually he'd look up.

'Dad! Dad!' I'd shout and wave. 'Daaaaaad!' When he saw us, he'd wave and smile.

'See you for dinner at six.' Mum would wave the fish in his general direction. Dad would nod. And we would walk home, mission accomplished.

*   *   *   *

Tugging on my Dad's sleeve, I picked up a cluster of pound notes. Excited about the sweets I could buy with £5, a huge amount to a young child, I asked Dad to take me to the shop.

'No. They belong to someone,' he explained. 'Let's hand them in to the police station.'

No amount of whining changed his mind. A few hot summers later, he would take my older sister, Harriet, and me swimming. A gaggle of friends would tag along, and Dad would walk from house to house, ensuring he had every parent's permission before we were allowed to clamber into the stifling car. My dad was always eager to do the right thing.

But I needn't have worried that day as I clutched greedily at my treasure; a week later no one had come forward, and Dad took me to the sweet shop to claim my prize. Heading home, he nipped into the off-licence to pick up four cans of Special

Brew along with two packets of Skips for my sister and me. This was his daily routine.

He had another routine, too.

Dad had erected a water butt in one corner of what we called the 'covered way' – a narrow corridor that ran alongside the house through to the garden. A piece of corrugated plastic stretched over the top made for shelter in the harshest of weathers. The water butt masqueraded as a coffee table, and here Dad would sit, in an armchair, beer and fags close to hand. He would spend his evenings alone, soothing himself to sleep with the noxious cocktail of nicotine and booze.

'David, David! Wake up. What are you doing?'

The buoyancy I felt over my 'sweet victory' was shattered that evening as my mum began shouting at my dad to get up and come inside. Why was she treating my dad like this? Why all the nagging? Why couldn't she just leave him alone? Walking out to the covered way, I saw my dad slumped in the chair while my mum paced around indoors.

'Come on, Dad, get up.' Shaking him awake, I tried to help him up.

'What are you shouting for?' Dad let rip a torrent of abuse at Mum.

'You're upsetting George. Can't you stop it?' she yelled back. 'Look at how much you're upsetting your son!'

Always concerned to protect me, Mum worried constantly about how I was affected. Frustrated and disappointed, I helped my dad upstairs. Dad and I were men together and I didn't need her protecting me. I wanted to be treated like the man I thought I was. Helping Dad out of his wet, sodden clothes, the smell was overpowering, but I didn't mind –

times like this were precious. These were the times when our conversations were deep, his thoughts flowed freely, and we were father and son.

Clean and dry, I could sink my face in his chest, the fibres of his jumper tickling my nose, a certain aroma now filling my senses; Old Spice; my dad the gentleman.

Born in North Finchley, his parents had instilled in him good manners, the importance of treating people well and doing the right thing. As a small boy he was sent to boarding school, an environment which for a gentle disposition was difficult to cope with. His father would drive to the school and take him, along with one or two friends, out for dinner. This was eagerly anticipated, so Dad became popular as a means to exit the grounds and the stodgy school food.

Despite boarding school, Dad had a close relationship with his parents, and would always speak well of them. However, at 17, after a big row with his father in the car, Dad got out, slammed the door and stormed off. That was the last time he saw his dad. On arriving home, my grandfather, only in his fifties, had a fatal heart attack. My dad was left to care for his mother.

Sniffing more deeply, there was the distinct aroma of offices – the photocopier ink, the dust of machines. For my dad, politeness and gentility were always important. He worked hard, he worked long hours, he cared. But a sense of failing at work, along with the pain of his father's death, drove him into himself, fearing life and questioning who he was.

He would take me to work with him, sometimes. Dad and me, men together, my mate. As he set to work on the computers, I'd fiddle around with whatever I could find – paper clips, Post-it notes. Very little amusement for a little kid, an office filled with machines, desks, paper. Everywhere seemed grey and lifeless, until the day I discovered my object of desire and affection. And after that, I would pay regular homage to the god of beverages. The drinks machine on the top floor sported over a hundred options, a towering epitome of liquid satisfaction. There were hot chocolates, teas, squashes, fizzy drinks. And they were free. But the Old Spice on Dad's skin and the smell of hard work could never overpower the lingering alcohol on his breath, his hands, his hair.

As a young man Dad had joined a rowing club where he discovered drink. They'd have a beer, he'd have a beer, and he could relax, away from the stresses of home and work. Alcohol freed him from his fears and allowed him to be himself. Even as a child, I longed that Dad would stop drinking so he could just be the good man I knew he was. I wanted Mum to see him like that; and as I got older, I wanted them to be in love, as they once had been.

Dad, at 21, had been invited by his friend to a party at his home. In the corner, gentle notes seeped from a piano. Mum caught his eye as her fingers delicately brushed the keys. As he sat down next to her on the stool, his hands joined hers, drawn into her rhythm, playing along. Dad married Mum two years later. Sensitive and kind, Mum's troubled childhood drew my dad into an emotional world. Eager to help, he spent hours listening, soothing, wiping away tears.

* * * *

I spent one of my childhood Christmases in bed. That was always the problem with school, other kids giving you their germs and spoiling your Christmas. I remember hugging the toilet bowl, whimpering as I was sick yet again; I was in Darley Dale in Derbyshire, at my gran's, holed away while the festivities continued without me.

The scenes were of Mum's childhood; hills of patchwork beauty and winding lanes to splash through when it rained, and vast canopies of spread-eagled greenery, glowing with sunlight, to seek shade under during summer, crisp and sprinkled with frosty whiteness at Christmas. Visits to my gran were frequent and much desired. Most weekends would see us bundled in the car, up and down the M1, the changing scenery reflected in the objects my sister and I would spell out in our I-Spy tournaments.

'I spy with my little eye something beginning with I T H M E N G H.' I'd try to outwit her, prove myself.

'You can't do that. I'll never get it.'

We'd get on sometimes but, nearly five years Harriet's junior, I was her annoying little brother. Once she slapped me so hard there was a mark on my face for days. I probably deserved it.

Family holidays are always good for memories. Freckle-decked faces, my sister, Harriet, and I would spend hours on the beach, and my dad and I would spend hours playing pool. I remember once, packing the car to leave for France, my father's face was unshaved, stubble poking through flesh, between red, raw streaks. My sister and I exchanged glances. We'd seen it, heard it, tried to make sense of it. The shouting; the alcohol always being the disembodied enemy that drove my parents to scream – and my mother, the night before, to hit out at my dad, scraping her nails down his face. Those two weeks in France were a blur of sun, sea and playing pool with my dad, punctuated by the vivid image of his ever-growing beard. A beard he never did get rid of, hiding the shame.

Wafts of turkey and potatoes drifted upstairs, and the noise of laughter reverberated through the floorboards that Christmas as I lay bored, listless and not really feeling that bad now my stomach was empty. I imagined the chocolate coins my sister was tucking into, the ice cream and the puddings. A now-empty stocking hung at the bottom of my bed; toys were scattered around the floor, and bits of wrapping paper, bright, gaudy in its nonsense, lying where it had been thrown. Some of my toys lay on Harriet's bed, a sneaky swap done in the early hours of the morning, covert, agreed, understood.

I picked away at the woodchip wallpaper, little flecks of wood coming off in my hands, threatening to jam into my skin under my nails. Despite being told off, there were blank patches on the walls over the beds were my sister and I slept.

'How do you feel, George?' Mum had been coming up every hour to check on me as I got progressively grumpy.

'Hungry.'

The next time Mum came up the stairs there was one sausage on a plate. I remember that Christmas and the solitary sausage. I also remember the electric toothbrush I got as a gift, disappointing my ungrateful childish self. Like the year I got an ugly jumper. I found receiving gifts difficult; I still do.

But one year the gift was too bright, red and shiny for even me to be disappointed. As I hauled myself up atop the saddle, I grew three inches. I was cool, I was king of the road, I had arrived, I had a BMX bike. Never mind the fact I still needed stabilizers to stop me toppling into the kerb.

'Hi! What's your name?' As I whirled round Finch Close trying out my new wheels, another boy tagged along.

'George. What's yours?'

'Ross. Can I have a go on your bike?'

I wasn't sure; it was new after all. I traded in a turn on my bike for a new friend that January, as memories of Christmas were over and school loomed, ugly, dull and grey.

Later, Ross and I stood outside his front door.

'Can George come for tea?'

I twiddled my thumbs.

'OK. George, have you asked your mum?'

Tea at Ross's was weird. I'd not been for tea at anyone else's house. I didn't know that behind the seemingly same grey houses, everyone was different. We ate things I hadn't seen before, and I didn't like it much.

I'd made friends with other neighbours. They were the ones we had in Amersham, and the only memory I have of the rolling hills of Buckinghamshire. They looked after our cats while we were on holiday and fed them more than we did. I remember cats that were twice the size we had left. Huge, waddling, perfectly content obese cats.

Chapter 2

Friends

Other kids joined Ross and I as the months sped toward my 8th birthday, hanging out, playing in the streets, on small patches of grass; our playground. We'd kick a ball against the wall of a house; blank, detached, it cried out for games. But the couple who lived there didn't like children. They didn't like each other much, either. Sometimes you could hear their arguments through the wall as we kicked the ball, the thud-thud-thud breaking up the shouts, the verbal abuse, hurt and pain of lost love.

That was until one sunny day.

'Geeoooorge!'

I'd kicked the ball over their fence. No sooner had Ross expressed his indignation at me losing the ball (no one in their right mind asked the arguing couple for their ball back), then we heard it land. *Smash!* Scuttling up to the fence I peered over, just tall enough to see into the garden, the house. And there it was, my football, lying on the dining room table, having smashed through the window. Shards of glass glinted, leaving scratches in perfect mahogany.

'Ruuuun!'

As well as Ross, I had a friend called James. I loved going to James's; he had a computer like those my dad worked on, but better. Dad's were full of spreadsheets, databases, numbers, words, a dot-dot-dash of never-ending boredom. But James's had games. Pushing a little cassette into a slot, you'd press and hold down 'record' and 'play' together. The machine would screech and whirr as if it was complaining and about to explode and, twenty minutes later, the electronic dots of joy would appear. Grabbing a joystick you'd fire at coloured lights, pixelated aliens. Electronic and clunky, it provided endless hours of prehistoric fun.

If, by some series of strange events, the modern technology grew tiring, James had an astonishing array of board games; a tower of family-friendly, peeling-at-the-edges boxes, each bursting at the seams where boards and pieces hadn't been stored away in the correct slots. Little bits of plastic always found their way into the wrong game, dice were borrowed, a chess piece exchanged for a draught. They smelt musty and could tell stories, like old books, of the laughter, the tears and arguments of competition. I don't remember playing board games with my dad. I envied this display of family unity.

'Shall we go to yours now, George?'

My heart sank. If, finding yourself on my street, you also possessed the gift of observation, you would notice one house had a mattress propped up against the window; windows were always wide open, even in winter. If you were perceptive you may have concluded a child had wet the bed and the mother was lovingly airing it, having lifted it, dragged it from its frame and lugged it to the window, where fresh air and the warmth of a radiator might remove the dampness, the smell. You probably wouldn't guess that it was the mattress belonging to an adult man. My father.

It wasn't just the mattress that prevented me from bringing mates home for tea. It was the chair that Dad sat in, in the living room. When he wasn't in the covered way he was in that armchair, nodding off, snoozing as the alcohol took effect. Messages from his bladder did not reach his brain in time, so the smell permeated through the room, down the hallway, up the stairs. Sometimes it felt as if the whole house smelt of boozy urine.

There were nights I'd hear banging and crashing, a little bit of shuffling, a small amount of grunting. Throwing back my covers, I'd pad into the hallway just in time to see Dad, eyes shut, trousers down, relieving himself in the laundry basket, lost on the way to the toilet. I'd wake him and guide him to the bathroom. Even if he made it to the bathroom, he'd often miss, decorating the tiled floor in a way I, as a child, was supposed to do.

For my mum, the difficulties of living with an alcoholic husband and two young children was a huge pressure I always grossly underestimated. In the morning, my dad would apologize and my Mum would shout. Dad would try to make amends; breakfast, or a day out, or a note promising change. Mum would nag. To me, Dad was the innocent party; my gentle, kind Dad, of whom every memory is tainted by booze.

And so James's question, innocent in its asking, came shuddering into my heart in a way bad news impacts in its delivery.

'Er . . . shall we go to the park instead? I've got my ball in my bag.'

I was desperate to steer James away from the mattress, the laundry basket, the chair and the complex matrix of relationships behind our run-of-the-mill front door.

'Sure.'

Disaster averted. For now.

* * * *

It was one of those warm evenings, the kind that make your neighbours stoke up the barbecue and children are allowed to play out later, just to enjoy the last glimmering splinters of sunlit grass, swatting at the midges who love that time of day; slightly balmy, sticky, but cool enough not to be fried, as we were in noonday sun. The sky was that deep blue tinged with pink where the sun once was, and everything smelt of freedom, peace and serenity. A perfect evening for Dad to be in the covered way, Special Brew by his side. The evening was set up perfectly, cigarette smoke mingling with all those special scents of summer.

Having not yet been sent to bed, I ran into the kitchen, opening the fridge, looking for orange juice. I saw Dad's cans of Special Brew, chilling. Lined up like soldiers called to attention waiting for their special orders, they signified all those things I was beginning to despise about home. Being different, never having mates back, Mum's nagging, and all the insecurities and anger that swamped me; all the things I had no words for or understanding of as a child. I grabbed the orange juice and went back to my bedroom.

'Mum! Where's my compasses? I need to do some maths before school tomorrow,' I called out as I rifled through the mess piled on my floor.

'Wherever you last left them,' she replied.

Lifting up my maths homework, which required no equipment at all, I found the compasses and went back to the kitchen.

I eased the point of the compasses into the bottom of the Special Brew, urging the slow trickle to hurry up as it wended its way down the plughole. Turning on the tap, I performed a careful replacement; air for alcohol, water for air, waiting as bubbles came out, allowing more water in, bit by bit, until my special mission was complete. A sticking plaster over each small hole and the cans were popped back in the fridge. Satisfied, I felt I'd achieved something; a mixture of revenge, and helping my dad.

'Arrrghhhh!'

It wasn't long before I could hear Dad bellowing somewhere between the kitchen and the covered way. There were slamming doors, and demands to know who did this. Somewhere between his shouting, my instant realization of wrongdoing and my mum's getting involved, it became apparent to my parents that I was the culprit.

'George!' yelled my dad. 'Come here. Come here, now!'

'David, George just cares about you.' Trying to placate, Mum jumped to my defence. I'm not sure how that altercation ended. I just know I never did anything like that again.

While interrupted by many happy memories, the frustration of home, the constant feeling like I was the younger kid, and the overarching pain of seeing my dad descend into alcoholism, drove me out to find solace in family beyond those four walls.

The local woods and park became the place where I sought excitement, adventure and escape.

Chapter 3

Experiences

I took a big gulp. The cool, metallic-tasting liquid oozed down the back of my throat.

'George, you're not supposed to swallow it.'

My friend's voice sounded as if it had been passed through a distorter. I could hear bells, millions of pretty little bells that tinkled; the ends of my fingers and the tip of my nose were tingling. It felt as if my head was barely balancing on my shoulders. 'What have you done to your hair?'

As I stared at the pink spikes, I just couldn't fathom why Andrew would want to turn himself into a punk. Face pierced, tattoos on every available show of flesh, and wearing leather trousers, it was a dramatic transformation. I had no idea that the lighter fuel I had tipped into my mouth was causing me to hallucinate.

At 10, my first experience with lighter fuel unnerved me, excited me and made me feel confident and respected. By far the youngest of my group of friends, I could hold my own with the rest of them, just as I had been doing since I was 8. Back then, one sunny day in the park, my sister had asked, 'Do you want a fag?'

Harriet's question prompted feelings of excitement hard to resist. Because she was older than me, she always had the upper hand. As the youngest in the family I was the little brother that needed protecting, but I wanted to be taken seriously, to be respected. As Harriet held the packet towards me, this was my chance.

Coughing and choking, it felt as if my lungs were heaving their way through my throat. The taste of chemical ash filled my mouth, but I felt great. 'Don't inhale so deeply,' Harriet cautioned. 'Just suck it into your mouth.' This time it felt even better.

Andrew Fitzpatrick sauntered up to me later that day.

'I hear you started smoking?'

Andrew was in my sister's year at school. Grown up and cool, he embodied all I wanted to be, and now here he was, looking at me with approval.

'Yeah, I'm a smoker.'

I was hopeful my admission would secure me a high place in his estimation. It worked; from then on I got to hang out with the older lads, feeling respected and admired in a way I did not feel at home.

The following day, in order to secure my new status, I asked my sister for two more of her cigarettes. As the bell rang at 10:30 that morning, I sneaked into the school toilets with a packet of matches and my sister's forbidden fags. Sparking the match on the side of the box, my heart raced. Palms sweaty and fingers shaking, I lit the first cigarette and took a quick drag, desperately keeping my ears open for the sound of approaching footsteps. I took two puffs before the tension was too much and I flicked the cigarette to the floor and stamped it out. Gingerly I opened the cubicle door and peered around. There was no one there, so I sauntered out.

As the next lesson began, I whispered to my mate, 'I started smoking. I even do it at break.'

I repeated the process at lunchtime. From then on I considered myself a smoker and felt taller, older, stronger. It was exciting. I was now a man.

'It has come to our attention that someone is smoking in the boy's toilets,' thundered the headmaster, Mr Andrews, in assembly a few weeks later. 'This behaviour will not be tolerated. We will find out who the culprit is, but meanwhile, if you have any information, please come to my office.'

I sat at the back and trembled, my new-found manliness edging away as I realized how stupid I had been.

The queue to the headmaster's office stretched round the corridor that morning, filled with kids eager to let it be known that I was the perpetrator. I had not been particularly quiet or bashful in informing my schoolmates that I smoked at school, and they weren't bothered about keeping the information to themselves.

It wasn't long before I found myself face to face with Mr Andrews.

Pain hit my chest as Mr Andrews probed, his prodding finger enacting his desire to dig into my heart and discover truth. The evidence was stacked against me – it had lined the corridors all morning. There was no point denying it. I knew it, Mr Andrews knew it, and now my mother was going to know. I cried as I begged Mr Andrews to let me be the one to tell her.

Words were difficult that afternoon as I walked the familiar route home, all the while rehearsing my speech. It was Friday. Could I delay until Sunday night? But what of the rest of the weekend, the feelings of impending doom absorbed into every moment? Over and done with; that's the best idea, I decided. Picturing Mum, what would she say? Would she fly off the handle? Would I be punished? Mum was never predictable.

When she was growing up in Derby, there was to be a family photo taken in Matlock one warm, sunny afternoon. Mum was dressed in her best clothes, pigtails plaited and bowed. Then, taking a pair of scissors, she chopped the hair off, right to her scalp. She did the same to a friend at school during an art lesson – picked up her scissors, reached over, cut the pigtails off. Just like that. She was creative and headstrong, in contrast to her older sister who was perceived as favoured – 'Why can't you be more like your sister?' This instilled rebellion and insecurity in my mum, a quality which drew her to Dad, looking for salvation.

Once home, I sobbed as I formed that dreaded sentence and waited for the telling-off, feeling the overwhelming sense of being a disappointment.

'Why smoke at school?' Her question was gentle and unexpected and, speaking for themselves, my tears were the only punishment I needed. I was soon tucking into a banana sandwich.

Shortly after I started smoking, Andrew knocked on my door.

'You coming out?' he asked.

As I slipped on my coat and tied my laces, I felt proud that a 13-year-old would want to hang out with me. We sauntered through the back-to-back seventies-style houses, and through to the woods.

'This is Daniel, Marsella, Ruth, James and David. This is George.' Andrew introduced me to faces I recognized from the estate, and faces I recognized from my sister's school - all at least four years older than myself. Sitting around on logs in a small clearing, I desperately tried to make cool conversation and quick jokes.

Five years older than me and tall for his age, Daniel would collect our £2.20s. Where height and advanced development once meant bullying, it now signified income as he headed to the shop to buy us alcohol – and pocket the change.

'Here, George, try this.' Daniel chucked a bottle of cider in my direction. Eager to please, I took a big swig and looked for someone to pass it on to.

'It's all right, mate, it's all yours.'

I had no idea my £2.20 could buy a whole bottle of Merrydown cider, and I had no idea how I would drink it all. But I wanted to fit in. I took a deep breath . . . Draining the last drop, I knew my world had spun round, blurring at the edges. My body had altered and I struggled to keep face, to pass it off as OK; I was with it, a man. My stomach flipped and flopped, trees jiggled around in front of my face, and my new friends loomed frighteningly loud and then eerily quiet.

Somehow, I groped my way home. I have no recollection of that journey; I guess the familiar paths, cracks in the pavement, the uniform cars in driveways and the tree with the knobbly trunk were all etched on my subconscious, enough to guide me to safety. Acutely aware of my stomach churning, I remember running a bath, in a bid to feel better; I thought maybe the warmth of the water would soothe me.

Easing myself into the warm water, I retched, swallowed, and retched some more. Before I knew it, my bath of warm soapy water was a cesspit of cider-flavoured vomit. A heady concoction.

Having washed myself down, yet still aware of the stench of sick, I frantically tried to clean the bath, quietly, now far more sober, willing all the vomit to go down the plughole, shoving at it with my fingers, squishing it down. I was desperate for Mum to not find out. Satisfied I had done a good job, I went to bed. I may have had an ordeal, but at least Mum wouldn't know.

I woke the next morning to another sea of vomit. On my face, the pillow, the duvet. Head pounding, body shuddering, I groggily tried to formulate a plan to move, to clean, willing my limbs up and out. But the door opened, and Mum walked in . . .

As drink and cigarettes became boring, my reputation as the one who would try anything – 'Here, George, try this' – grew over the next couple of years.

Once Andrew had stopped looking like a punk that day, two years later, and I was over the fear that I'd feel abnormal forever, the logs in the small clearing set the stage for a whole theatre of excitement in my young life.

*   *   *   *

Carefully I popped open the small leather pouch James had passed me in the lane.

'You better save me some of that, George, for all the times you've had stuff off me,' he'd said.

I'd handed over the cash, stolen from Gran's purse earlier that day – she'd come to stay with us. I remembered sliding my hand in, heart racing, desperate to get what I wanted: £15. All the while she was busy making me a cup of tea, and finding a chocolate digestive. Kindly, gently, grandmotherly.

I hated that lane, running adjacent to the woods on the one side and our estate on the other. The park sat at the bottom. Darkness enveloped it, as a cloud of fear; very few cars broke the silence or the gloom. Night made it perfect for our covert operation.

And now, there it was, and I was proud. No longer did I have to take stuff off my friends; no longer did I have to ask or be offered. Mine. Purchased in the darkest of nights. Light and brown, a piece of 'slate', all ready to be held over a flame until it fluffed up and spread out, appearing as its namesake. Crumple it up, put it in a Rizla and you have a joint of cannabis. I thought I'd arrived.

Days, weeks, months passed as a blur. Spending hours in Marsella's house, sometimes three of us, sometimes a crowd, we'd smoke joints, drink beer. It was there I got introduced to the bong, a smoking apparatus constructed from bowls, tubes and water. The resulting smoke was cool, inhalation deeper, the high faster. Not all my mates would smoke the bong. As usual, I was the one singled out to try it by Marsella's older brother. A 'whitey' was a common experience – making you sheet pale, sick. Sitting for hours in a bathroom while waves of nausea crashed over me, threatening to erupt into the toilet bowl, never seemed to be a waste of my time. When the bongs were out or joints passed round, masks dropped off. We were us, really us. Say what you think, what you feel. Move with the moment. We were family, and I belonged.

*   *   *   *

'You are the youngest person I have ever had in my station.'

Looking down at my feet, I wiggled, colour creeping from my toes to my cheeks and settling atop my ears. Desperately wanting to appear unconcerned, I suddenly felt every bit the child. A strange feeling of vulnerability, of exposure, that I'd not felt in a long time . . . I'd been caught out.

Leaving Marsella's house, we'd decided to catch a bus. I don't know where we were headed, but it didn't matter; we had what we wanted, what we needed, and that was enough.

There was always plenty of banter, pushing, shoving. One minute you were the victim, cast to the edge by sneering faces and cutting remarks, but within seconds, the focus was off you and onto another. The cause of hilarity and weed-induced giggles had no rhyme or reason; the focus would shift as fast as the flip of a coin.

There must have been seventeen of us at that bus stop in Knaphill that evening. We weren't doing anything unusual. But within seconds they were on us. We were trapped, caught, searched. That evening the police found LSD, hash, trips and pills.

'We're going to need something bigger down here.' The sergeant spoke into his walkie-talkie.

'How many?'

'Seventeen, teenagers.'

I'd lied about my age, told the sergeant I was 13. I was easily believed in those days; my healthy appetite meant I looked older than my years.

'Right, everybody onboard. Keep your hands where we can see them.'

'Hands on the chair in front, ladies and gentlemen.'

We followed the police instructions, trying not to laugh as we clambered aboard the little bus. It pulled away from the bus stop and, as if we were a group of classmates off on a school trip, a museum, a zoo or a youth hostel awaiting us, the hilarity became a little too much.

'Quiet! Hands where we can see them.' The sergeant repeated himself, losing his patience at our sniggering, our complete inability to take the situation seriously.

Arriving at Woking police station, we were separated. The girls were strip searched – something that caused a number of issues with parents for days to come. There were some threats, some yelling, but nothing ever happened, nothing was ever resolved. We were all released within a few hours. My parents were never called. But within a few days, they had found out by some mysterious means, and marched me down to the police station.

'Do you know how old he is?' they said. 'He's 11.'

That was how I came to be having a drugs lecture from an inspector in Woking police station. And how I came to be known as the youngest person he had ever had there.

My dad had been enough for my mum to deal with up until this point. I was an added extra, a burden of guilt. After this, my parents began to take more interest in me. Mum would want to know where I was going, when I'd be back, whereas before I had had untold freedom.

Eventually, the summer was over. Secondary school beckoned. Easing into life as the youngest in the school was daunting. But having friends in the top year meant any fight I was in was quickly resolved. I always won. I was that kid that every parent was afraid of their child mixing with; the one that had already tried everything, had already latched on to the thrill-seeking roller-coaster.

I was determined not to keep these experiences to myself.

Chapter 4

My Young Life

'Rob, Lucy, Michael.' The teacher called out lists of names, directing us to various form groups, one by one. As every child stood up and moved around the hall, I sized them up.

'Michael?'

Michael stood up, nervously. He was small, with blond curtained hair flopping, obscuring his view. Slightly crumpled, faded, the 'passed down' effect appeared round the edges of his uniform. Not at all intimidating. Friend material, I considered.

'Rob?' Naturally rugged but all ironed out in a bid to control tufts of wavy hair, Rob moved with confidence. Someone to be seen with.

'George?' The walls dropped away, the ceiling stretching up. Faces stared as I stood, heart racing. All those eyes – what did they see as they looked at me? Someone to like? The tough guy I wanted to be? I had nothing to hide behind. I was nobody.

They shut the school gates at 8.30 a.m. One morning, glancing nervously at my watch, I knew I was going to miss it; I was late. Trouble with authority was something with which I would become familiar, even comfortable; but back then I was new, still eager to please. Going round the front of the building and signing in late felt overwhelming.

Arriving at the locked school gates, I sized them up. Could I? Would I?

'They're not that high.'

I took a breath and ran, leaping, grappling, hands clawing at metal, muscles straining under my weight. Throwing my legs over the top, I landed, synchronized with the most enormous 'rrrrrrrrrrrrriiiippp'. I looked down. Around my ankles were the remnants of my trousers, completely torn apart at the seams.

'Oh, George, what have you done?'

I found a teacher in the staff room while my year group were in PE.

'They . . . they sort of ripped.'

'OK, well, we'll have to get you home for some new ones. Come with me.' Following Mr Brown, I shuffled along, head bowed. At one point, glancing up, I caught the faces in the proudly displayed wall-mounted school photos. Every single one of them seemed to be laughing at me. But worse was to come. I had to walk past the school hall where the wall was made from glass, and my form group were in the middle of assembly.

The replacement trousers I found for myself at home were too tight and too small, leftovers from primary school. I spent the rest of the day totally mortified.

Once my first week at Winston Churchill secondary school had passed, and form S3 became home, I began to establish myself as an 'it' guy. Smuggling cigarettes and escaping to the boundaries of the school grounds, I drew a crowd round me. My peers were easily encouraged to pull nicotine through pre-teen lungs; it saw us through maths and double geography. I guess we were all drawn to the excitement of being on the edge, part of a crowd. Rob and Michael became close mates to cling to and drag into my world of pleasure-seeking highs.

I hated PE. I loathed the tight shorts I had to wear, the showers after a vigorous game of rugby; I hated my body. In those sober moments I could see what the weed, booze and general misery were doing to me; I was getting fat. Sugar sandwiches were a favourite. Hiding myself away in my bedroom, I'd switch the TV on and sit and consume a pile of sugary bread. Or I'd buy a stack of chocolate bars on my way home from school, ramming them into my face as *Newsround* turned into *Blue Peter*, then *Neighbours* and the *News* – at which point I'd flick through the channels. If I wasn't smoking with my mates, I'd line my evening up TV programme by TV programme, food by food. I'd avoid downstairs; family dinners were out; I'd only surface to grab more food. Sometimes, though, we'd go out for dinner as a family. It seemed to be our way of expressing family time, Dad's way of treating us.

* * * *

'Here, Rob, try this.'

Rob took the spliff. 'Mum's gonna kill us.' His mum already disliked me; I was hurt by this, but I didn't see at the time that I, the ringleader, was leading her son down paths filled, for her, with fear; although he went willingly.

I blinked. For hours I'd been transfixed, playing a racing game, consumed by the trance music raging from the speakers, images of cars spinning down tracks. Every moment I was the driver, turning, upside down, the track flying under me as I gripped the wheel, willing the car to go faster. But with just one blink I was free, and my stomach growled.

'Rob, let's get something to eat.'

'Mum's around, though, mate.'

Those moments were weird; we only wanted a sandwich, but the paranoia of being caught when we were high turned every movement into an operation, a secret mission.

'Check the landing, mate.'

'Clear!'

'Let's go,' I said. Every wall was our cover, every piece of furniture our bunker as we sidled our way to the kitchen, our senses on high alert, our bodies freezing at every sound.

'Shhhh! She's just through there.' Rob pointed to where his mum was on the phone in the living room, chatting away as she flicked through a magazine, a cup of tea on the little table by the sofa.

Creaking open the fridge, I reached for the butter.

"All right, boys?"

I froze. Rob's mum had appeared, grabbed a biscuit from the cupboard, and walked out again. Scrambling for fillings, bread, a knife, we shoved everything on a plate and pelted through the kitchen up the stairs, and back into Rob's room. There we collapsed in a fit of giggles. Mission accomplished! Breathing a huge sigh of relief, I sank my teeth into a peanut butter sandwich.

* * * *

I considered my weapon. Little nails jutted through an old pair of shin pads, strapped tightly round my legs, over jeans. Rob tucked a knife into his coat pocket, and we sneaked from the kitchen when his mum was in the other room.

'Ready?'

'Let's do this!' Rob opened the back door and we slipped out.

He had his hand protectively on his pocket, almost afraid the knife would vanish, slip out – or worse, he would be caught unprepared, needing to whip it out, use it. I imagined the blade glinting, the flesh it would sink into; our ultimate weapon, our final protection. And my shin pads, the spikes cutting through the jeans of another, scraping, clawing, tearing. We were ready.

'This way, George.'

I followed Rob round the corner of Finch Close, and we went to the park, ducking behind trees, peering out, running for the next, always under cover. We couldn't be seen or caught.

'Quickly, George.' Always a few steps behind, the weight of evenings watching TV and eating sugar sandwiches slowed me down. Smoke-tarred lungs choked oxygen from my veins. I hurried, knowing our plan could not fail, must not fail. I checked my shins; my weapon was still intact, and knowing Rob had the knife reassured me.

And then it was over. We had succeeded.

Leaving the newsagent, I clutched at my Mars Bar and slurped my coke. No one had attacked us. We were safe. Yes, we really did need to be 'tooled up' just to go to the local shop.

The really daring escapades, those that took the day to psyche ourselves up for, to get really high in preparation, were those where we ran out of giant Rizla papers and needed to ask for more. Would the shopkeepers know? Could they tell? What would they do to us, with us, if they figured it out? But there was pride in a 'rollie', and only the giant Rizla would do. My rollies were the best, I always knew that.

We would watch TV in those days and think the people on it were talking to us – the men in the box, the women dressed to impress, far away.

'Why did he just say that? That man?' It was the paranoia talking. The same paranoia that drove us to run to shops with weapons. Our top-secret chocolate and Rizla missions.

'Look how fat that woman is, Rob.' I'd laugh at a large woman on the TV and immediately be gripped by anxious thoughts: Does she think I'm fat, too? Does Rob? What about that man in the picture frame – is he staring at me?

Cycling home on those nights in the dark, lights out on my bike, I was at risk, but I didn't realize it. As I lost control and once again found myself in a ditch, grass up my nose, mud smeared across my face, in uncontrollable giggles, I really couldn't have cared less. I found myself hilarious.

My first year at Winston passed like this; a gaining of momentum in friendships, misdemeanours and any substance I could get my hands on.

Days at home were spent in the garden. The weeping willow in the back garden looked beautiful that summer, its long fingers drooping, tickling the grass below. I could still exert childish enthusiasm and, despite being encumbered by my weight, climb its tangled branches. I remember having just returned from a holiday in Darley Dale, Dad had been out mowing the lawn. He'd also been at the stove, filling the air with the smell of bacon and eggs.

My memories of the Darley Dale holiday that year are bathed in sunshine. Dad and I had been to the Corn Exchange to play some pool. He'd had a sneaky beer while I potted colour after colour until just the black remained, the gateway to victory. I'd balanced the cue carefully, slowly, intentionally positioned. Pull it back, green end striking the white, white hitting the black . . . and disappearing out of sight, far corner. Inside I soared. But the real prize was the time spent with Dad, laughing, chatting, being men. Holidays tend to suspend reality; it was all smiles and laughter. Sadly, alcohol refused to play along with the rules, refused to be polite, well-mannered. As the booze came out so did sharp words so out of place with summertime, ice creams and grandmothers' houses.

Alcohol was always the intruder, the unwelcome guest at any party. Before secondary school days, parents' evenings were intensely important. Mum and Dad would attend parent-teacher social evenings; it was their way of being involved. But they would always end with Dad slumped on a table amongst empty glasses and dishes, face buried in his arms, breathing heavily. The other parents would step round him, ignore him, pretend he wasn't there – pretend 'it' wasn't there. And the holidays in Darley Dale would end the same way, too; especially at Christmas – Dad lolling around in an armchair in an alcohol-induced stupor. Mum's frustration would ooze from every pore, disrupting the holiday peace.

'Penny, leave the poor man alone.' Mum's sister would see Mum as the problem, unaware of the constant pain, difficulty and embarrassment.

I was a chip off the old block. One of the weekends that bordered the six weeks of lazy summer days, we drove down to Torquay. You'd turn a corner and there was the sea stretched out, walled by cliffs, stacked high with white houses glinting in the sunshine. The harbour was filled with boats yanking at their anchors and ropes, wind whistling through masts. Beaches were filled with overly toasted holidaymaking Brits, children building empires from the red, clay-soaked sand while dads dug out cars and speed boats, and mothers watched nervously as those old enough to swim slipped in and out of waves. Seagulls would dart around, desperate to steal your sandwiches, your ice cream.

During the summer, Torquay was a noisy explosion of childlike colour, resplendent in its display of tacky shops, tourist attractions, boat trips and burnt tourists; the Great British seaside resort. Off season, the wind buffeted the sand across pavements, and the white houses stood casting nervous eyes at the threatening sea, which crashed over the walls. Devoid of entertainment and excitement, the teenagers were bored.

The friends who had made our cats fat in Amersham had relocated to the coast. Our visits were frequent and educational.

'Hey, George, you tried a shotty?'

A shotty was like a bong, but with a special metal tube to suck out of. There was pride in these metal tubes; they were carefully bought, crafted, taken care of, experienced.

Packed with weed, they were inserted into a vessel at an angle below the water level, once the draw was lit. Toking on the metal tube you'd hear a loud whooshing, popping sound, as smoke would shoot into your mouth; an instantaneous high.

'Hey, George, pass the shotty, mate.'

I leaned over, arms dangling from windows as I passed it to our mate in another car. There were three or four vehicles parked up in the dark, deserted car park that Saturday evening. Our parents were oblivious to what we were up to; they were happy that we were friends, enjoying each other's company. It was a new kind of freedom. In those days, one of my mate's mums would pick him up from school with cigarettes in the car, ready to hand over to him. Bring a child into the world, encourage their exit by lung disease. But back then I was jealous.

Backwards and forwards the shotty flew, car to car, seat to seat, front to back. My head was lolling around my shoulders as the music pounded, taking me captive. The car radio was all lit up and sparkly, like a cottage at night. No, it *was* a cottage. The radio had windows, four of them, and a door. There was even a little light, illuminating the front. My mate pressed the eject button, popping the tape from the player, switching to radio.

'Nooooo!'

'No way, man!'

'That's crazy.' The tape had been playing the same song as the radio station we switched to. It was surreal. The bizarreness of it all unnerved me, the familiar paranoia creeping round the edges of my otherwise enjoyable high.

I took some shotties back to Woking, delighted that I could introduce something new to the group.

The irony was, though, that that summer I wanted things to be different. 'Something has to change, Dad,' I told him. 'We need to sort this out. Mum loves you.' I wanted Dad to be better. His reply was full of love for Mum, and the desire to do things right.

And so Dad wrote a contract with my sister. A few words, a scrap of paper, taped to his wall for a couple of weeks – promises to stop drinking for three months. It was an honest, heartfelt desire to do what was right, starting with the cut grass and the fried breakfasts.

Chapter 5

Spirits . . . and Sex

As summer faded into autumn, my dad's good intentions faded too. The garage door, with its grey undercoat on, seemed a promise of better things to come. But it was a lost promise; an unfinished job. Just as Dad was back in the covered way, so I was back at school feeling the pressure of home life, and with a reputation to uphold.

The evenings held their light way beyond the end of school, and the weekends would stretch out lazily, giving us time to do nothing. On those September weekends, Goldsworth Park became the hang out place of choice. Sometimes just one friend and I, sometimes the whole crew. In one corner of the park stood a function hall, the Goldwater Lodge, used for low budget affairs; weddings, golden anniversaries, 18th birthdays. A few balloons, a cold buffet, a drunk uncle or two and you'd almost be mistaken for thinking it was a venue worth spending money on.

'Hey, George, shall we go see what's happening in the hall?'

It had become a pastime for us, sneaking in, looking around, pretending to be Sandra's cousin, Betty's half-brother, the other person's friend. The chill of autumn was in the air; today was the last wedding of the summer season.

We walked in. The drunken uncle, swaying and lewdly eyeing up the ladies could only mean one thing – the alcohol was flowing, and we wanted in. I walked to a table, nonchalantly, pretending I belonged, was known; I picked up a beer and downed it. The others did the same. Soon, though, what we were doing became obvious.

'What do you think you're doing? Get out!'

As the fog of alcohol descended, focusing on being natural became too hard an act; rowdiness, disorderliness and shouting blew our cover.

'Right, that's it!' yelled someone. 'I'm calling the police.'

I woke up with my mum standing over me in a cell in Woking police station. Dad wasn't there; he was too drunk to function. Like father, like son.

'Mum, I want a cup of tea.' She didn't have to be in the cell with me; she could have waited upstairs. Too drunk to notice her love, I demanded, 'Tea, Mum!' and I hung my finger on the buzzer.

'Sit down, George,' Mum pleaded.

'You can't tell me to sit down.' I kept buzzing, then hammering, fists pounding the door, alcohol removing any sense of pain.

'I want a cup of tea. Get me tea!' I roared.

I had to go back to the police station a few days later for the inspector to tell me off and issue a caution.

'Look what you're doing to your parents. Do you feel proud?' The inspector knew, he saw, he understood.

'I'll stop drinking when Dad does.'

'Don't do as I do,' Dad said. But I felt no guilt or shame before my father; there was nothing to look up to, and no one to please. Embarrassment vaguely tinged the edges of my indifference. Still, I'd got away with it and life went on.

* * * *

It was wet and awkward; something akin to sucking the last bits of pulp from an orange quarter at half time during a rugby game. Dad would take me to rugby games, cheer from the side, look like a normal dad. He'd hand me my water, pat me on the back, tell me I'd done a good job when the game was over. We enjoyed sports together, Dad and I. But this was altogether different. I felt like I'd let myself down, let her down; I really didn't know what I was doing.

'All right, then, George. See ya, then.' Kathy walked off with a toss of her hair, a casual wave and a glance over her shoulder as she disappeared into her house.

'See ya!' I called after her. It certainly wasn't romantic and I definitely wasn't cool. But it was what it was, my first kiss.

Kathy was the kind of girl that had had loads of boyfriends before me. I knew I wasn't special, but to be chosen, despite the fact that she was working her way round the class, made my heart soar. I made out she wasn't the first, that I, too, was in demand. I expect my orange sucking approach to our first kiss gave me away.

Kathy's mum was doing the best she could to raise a family without a husband. Out at work for most of the day, the house was empty for us to come and go, grab food, play computer games. Every time we hung out, there would be the big event, the kiss. I'd wait for it, build up to it. Then it would happen; empty and quick, we'd wave goodbye, no depth of knowing.

We were supposed to leave the door of the back room open when we were in there together, but we never would. Rolling around on the sofa, kissing would lead onto other things – first experiences of what a girl was like, and what it felt like to be physically involved with someone; not that we went 'all the way' at that stage. But I still didn't really know who Kathy was, other than my first girlfriend.

'BRRRRIINNGGG!'

My dad would ring the doorbell, ready to take me home.

'See you, Mrs Jones!' I would yell as I slipped out, red-faced, to where my dad was waiting.

Around this time the weed, alcohol and lighter fuel began to lose their rush, becoming old news. What had started out as a giggling bundle of amusement, a bit of weed stuffed in a rollie, had become a quiet pyramid of paranoia and fear that was getting me into trouble. Landing in a police station wasn't fun, and the horrendous hangovers were becoming a little mundane. I was ready for something more, something better. Adrenalin, my drug of choice, needed new catalysts, different triggers.

Rumbling round school there was a whisper, an idea gathering speed, forming understanding. Like the facts of life, you hear, you learn, you piece the information together until you can join in the conversation with confidence. 'Ouija board' carried this status. I watched from the sidelines when they first did it at Rob's house. I saw the board, the glass, the huddle, the hands. I felt the chill, the wonder, the disbelief. I was intrigued and I knew this was next. It was for me.

We'd never do it at my house. The mattress propped against the window, a sign of what lay behind – Rob understood.

Over beers, perched on his bed, we'd talk of our dads, beginning to make sense of what our eyes had seen, but youth, until now, had rendered us incapable of understanding.

One afternoon, Rob reached into his black chest of drawers. 'Want to play some Oujia?'

Lifting the lid of the battered box, Rob whipped the board out and placed it nonchalantly on the top of another piece of his regulation teenage bedroom furniture. He left me alone in the room while he ran downstairs to find a glass, and let Michael in the front door.

The board was unremarkable in its appearance, nothing more than a few words and numbers on thickened card, but it had already intrigued me. The sound of Rob and Michael's teenage banter and heavy feet on the stairs quickened my already galloping heart.

Clustering round the board, Rob placed the glass on the centre.

'Use your little fingers, then we'll know it's the spirits, not us,' Michael said as we reached out to the cool glass, slightly sweaty, yet not really believing.

'Spirits . . . are you there?'

Almost immediately the air seemed to drop, somehow, closing in, weighty. I didn't dare ask if the others could feel it, fearing losing the moment, the magic.

Motion jogged my little finger. Moving the glass outwards towards the faded 'yes', I looked at Rob and Michael, breaking the silence.

'Was that you? Did you push it?'

They shook their heads. We stared at each other, suspicious.

'Are you a good spirit?' Michael ventured. His question provided no movement.

'Are you a bad spirit?' Our shaking little fingers moved slowly from 'yes' to 'no'.

'Maybe it *is* our fingers pushing it,' I said. 'Are you sure you didn't push that?'

We didn't dare remove ourselves, or shut the board. Slightly afraid, curious, we were still full of weighty disbelief.

'Who are you?' Rob wanted to continue, keep testing. This time the glass sped across the board spelling a word: 'J', 'O', 'H', 'N'. I couldn't have made that up and I knew the others wouldn't have thought of it. More questions followed, probing, wanting to know more of this spirit, who he was, his story. Questions to get to know someone who was dead quickly changed into a desire to know the future, believing the dead would be able to supply the information.

'G', 'O', 'O', 'D', 'B', 'Y', 'E'. Just like that, the spirit left. Air pushed itself into my lungs like I'd been under water too long. I gasped. The feeling in the room lifted.

'Shall we go for a fag?' Standing at Rob's back door, watching the last of the afternoon sunshine fade, rivulets of smoke rising, we comforted ourselves with the get-out clause that maybe we moved the glass. Deep down, though, we knew we hadn't.

'F', 'A', 'M', 'I', 'L', 'Y'. Perched on the stools in Rob's kitchen, the questions came fast, building to this revelation of identity. Christmas was rapidly approaching, frost frequented the grass, and it was dark by the time I'd get home from school. The central heating was rarely off, warming windswept, ice-tingled noses. But with the 'y' came an instantaneous drop in temperature akin to opening the back door. But the door was firmly shut and the thermostat routinely raised. I shivered.

'Are you my grandmother?' A gentle slide to the 'no'.

'Are you my grandfather?' I asked, and we watched as our little fingers slid to the 'yes'. Wide-eyed, Rob stared at me. After a couple of months playing with the board, we no longer asked the question – but I hadn't influenced the glass. Was Rob messing with me?

'Tell me what age my dad was when he had an argument with you just before you died.' That was a question Rob couldn't answer, family history he didn't know. The answer came immediately, accurately. I was hooked.

Clutching a photo of my grandfather, I approached the board with excitement the following day. As he answered questions about his appearance, I was convinced I knew who I was talking to. He could tell me things about my family that only the inner circle of relatives could know, and it wasn't long before he was revealing my future.

When it wasn't my grandfather, other 'dead people' (as we thought they were) would spell out their names, giving their occupation. Soldiers killed in various wars – World War I or World War II, sometimes older battles from centuries past – would 'appear' to us and tell us things. We'd ask for dates and figures, historical facts that we had no clue about. We'd jot them down, or remember them for later when we could check the data, and discover that they were telling the truth. Sometimes it was like being at school; history lessons being brought to life, where I hadn't listened in class. Their accuracy deepened the hold these things had over us. Why wouldn't anyone be fascinated and drawn in by this? And that was how I was told my mum would end up in a wheelchair; confined there for the remainder of her days. Even with the passing of years, and change of understanding, in the back of my mind I still have a niggling fear that that moment will come.

This became our daily routine. We'd often try to reconnect with spirits we'd talked with before. Chatting to one spirit at the beginning could quickly switch into talking to someone else, their personality discernible by the movement of the glass. Fast, slow, aggressive, gentle – little things giving us clues to the nature of the spirit. Like friends on the telephone, we never doubted their communication or their goodness. We relied on them to tell us what we wanted to know, believing their link to the future, all the while fascinated by voices from the grave.

*   *   *   *

The girls in the group were passed round much like a spliff, a fag or a bottle of cider. For now, I was still with Kathy and Rob was with Charlotte, but it wouldn't be long before we'd swapped, or moved onto someone new.

'Shall we do it tonight, George?'

'Yeah, sure, if you want.'

'Do you want to? '

'Yeah, OK.'

Losing my virginity at 12 years old was initiated by a semi-awkward, depth-free conversation.

'I'll get the condom if you like,' I said.

'See you tonight, then, George.'

Marcella's party was in full flow by the time Rob and I arrived.

'All right, mate?' Slaps on the back, handshakes, a grabbing of beer, cider. Music pulsated through the house; Marcella's mum was out, as usual. Lights were turned low and the air was heavy with the smog of cannabis, teenage sweat and expectation. All the crew were gathered. I could make out silhouettes in the dim light, nodding and saying hello as black blurs became recognizable. Tucked away in my inside pocket were a couple of Durex. I felt like a man tonight.

I'd no idea what I was doing when I'd walked into the pharmacy that afternoon, trying to override my acute sense of childlike ignorance with a confident stride, surrounding myself with the aura of 'I've done this many times'. I'd stared at the array and choice ahead of me, and grabbed the most basic packet I could find. Seemed the most sensible thing to do.

Somewhere between the pharmacy and home, Rob had caught up with me. Somewhere between Rob catching up with me and our saying our goodbyes, we had decided to sleep with our girlfriends that night, at the same time, at Marcella's party.

Edging my way round the room, drinking in the smoke, letting the music and alcohol plump up my confidence, I found Kathy giggling with some of the other girls by the snacks in the corner of the living room. Her elbow rested on the sideboard displaying framed photos of Marcella as a child, in a plain dress and pigtails at school, along with faded pictures of unrecognizable adults from apparently every generation. These photos displayed the never-ending passing on of genes through the very thing that I, as a 12-year-old, felt was my right, my time.

'Hey, babe!' Kissing her neck, I slipped my arms round her waist, enjoying the feeling of expectation and manliness that finding her, grabbing her and pulling her towards me gave to me. 'Wanna go somewhere else?'

Hand in hand we slipped up the stairs to someone's empty room. Out of the corner of my eye, I saw Rob and Charlotte doing the same. This was it. This was my moment.

And it very closely resembled my first kiss.

'Gonna go find the girls,' Kathy said when it was over. Awkward, unromantic, yet kept sacred by the façade of cool nonchalance. Like this was all it was meant to be.

'Sure, babe. See you later.' Ceremoniously, I met Rob in the bathroom to flush away our condoms. Full of bravado, I kept my disappointment to myself and broke up with Kathy soon after, embarrassed by her knowing of me and the emptiness of unfulfilled intimacy.

*   *   *   *

Past the cornflakes and other cereals and round to the coffee – ground, beans, decaffeinated. I surveyed the alcohol aisle from a distance. No shop attendants or shoppers; the coast was clear. Slipping between the lines stacked high with wine, beer and spirits, I pulled the cigarette packet out of my pocket, and my two pence piece. I was going to ask the spirit world for some help. Lifting a bottle of vodka from eye-level height I whispered, 'Is anyone coming?' The queen's face on the coin shifted to the 'no' written on the cigarette packet. The vodka fitted neatly into the inside pocket of my huge jacket, and I crept out of the shop.

Like learning an art, a sport, a trick, once you become proficient, you can begin to gain an insight and understanding into a certain world and how it operates. Then you can learn to adapt and access the same knowledge and powers in a different way; a more efficient way. That was how the coin method had developed. I'd write 'yes' and 'no' on a cigarette packet, a slip of paper, or my hand, and the coin would move, indicating the answer. The spirit world was guiding my every decision, warning, encouraging, as I asked for insights.

Back at school I settled into my chair; in front of me were row after row of nervous teenagers. Papers had been placed on small desks, accompanied by see-through packets containing pens, pencils and calculators. Teachers on the stage were peering, waiting.

'You have exactly two hours. Turn your papers over and begin.'

Flicking open the exam booklet, I stared at the first question. Not a clue. I glanced over at Tracy, thinking of the times we'd sat, back row in German, her hands all over me, my hands all over her. Catching her eye, she shrugged.

In and out of a young offenders' prison all through this, our third year at Winston, Tracy was trouble. She broke into houses, got into fights; that risky behaviour attracted me, yet also scared me; it kept me on my toes, kept me looking up, growing up, becoming more manly. We belonged to different groups, but we'd kiss and mess around in the park, when our groups mingled, hanging on the swings, sharing stuff we'd nicked or got from the off-licence.

Under my desk, the queen's face was squished in my clammy hand, sandwiched between a 'yes' and 'no'. I whispered the question, the coin moved. Writing the answer on the line provided, I breathed a sigh of relief. It would be good to pass this exam.

In the weeks that followed, coins, cigarette papers and hands became a continual way of making decisions and discerning my future; where to go, the exact location of my mates, whether the coast was clear for smuggling unpaid-for goods from shops. The spirits guided me, controlled me.

'Why are we faffing around with all these bits of paper and coins?' Rob, Michael and I were in the kitchen, with cans of coke and the Ouija board out. 'Why don't we ask the spirits to come into us?'

I reflected; it was cumbersome trying to steal and juggle our occult devices simultaneously. We asked the spirit we'd been conversing with that afternoon if this were possible; could spirits inhabit humans? As the glass flew to 'yes', I picked it up. I pressed it to my ear and uttered what seemed to be appropriate words.

'Come into me, come into me.'

I had granted permission. I waited. Silence. Nothingness. Rob and Michael copied me. 'Come in to me, come in to me.' Putting the glass back in the cupboard we went off to the park for a kick around.

Rudely awoken by my alarm a few days later, I groaned. It was the middle of February, cold outside my duvet and dark beyond the curtains. Sleep-induced freedom from anxiety and confusion gave way to pressing thoughts within minutes of consciousness. I remembered a girl in my year at school, and all the spirits had led me to believe about our impending marriage. The trouble was, she was nice, but I didn't fancy her – and marriage? Besides, I'd been woken at 5 a.m. that morning by Tracy knocking on my window. Running the memory through my mind, I felt trapped and in despair. Climbing onto the garage roof below, crawling up to the wall of the house, most likely clinging on for dear life, Tracy would make her way to my window where she would knock and knock until I let her in, afraid Mum or Dad would hear. Sometimes I wished they would. We'd have sex before she hastily left again. All this felt a step too far for me; that and the police knocking on my door at random times, interrupting otherwise peaceful evenings, looking for her. I knew I had to end it.

Becoming more lucid as sleep ebbed away, I remembered the spirit's words about Mum – how would she end up in a wheelchair? Who would take care of her, and could I do anything to prevent it? Should I warn her? Downstairs raised voices mingled with the smell of toast. Suddenly I caught the word 'divorce'. Slamming of doors, feelings of déjà vu. In the back of my mind I heard a voice – not audible, but a forming of words, nonetheless. I knew which room my mum had just walked into. I knew that the shower was now free from my sister's plethora of products. I was told to get up.

Chapter 6

Deliverance

The evenings were getting lighter with the giving way of March into April. Dreariness no longer hung over the park like a forbidding cloud. Daffodils appeared through the sodden ground, and crocuses were everywhere. Feeling like the first day of warmth since last summer, people had come scurrying out of hibernation, peeling off layers of clothing. There'd been balls and frisbees flying through the air, screaming children on swings, lovers entangled on rugs. With the fading of the light, parents packed their children back into coats and led them away. Still too chilly to stay out beyond 5 p.m.; Saturday night television and takeaways beckoned.

'You called me a slut.'

'As if! I don't think that.' I tried to argue with Tracy, but I knew I wouldn't win. The evening may have been warm, but I half-wished I was in the safety of home, having just broken up with Tracy

'You told the police where I was. What is wrong with you?'

I genuinely had no idea what Tracy meant, but I knew one thing – she was angry and I was in trouble. We had only been going out for six months, but she was suffocating me and I was afraid of her, her mood swings, her forays with the police.

I wasn't interested in those games now; the spirit world was too intriguing.

'I'm going to kill you, George.' Where she got the iron pipe from I have no idea. Maybe it was from an old battered-down railing that ran around the park, the result of months of county council cuts, leaving public areas shoddy and unkempt; there were better things to spend time and money on. Or maybe it had been slung in that waste area where nothing much grew but nettles, covered by rubble and everyone's rubbish. Wherever it was from, I will not forget that mild evening, the crocuses popping out, the families happy in the spring sunshine, while I was chased around the town by my spurned ex-girlfriend brandishing a dangerous weapon.

I never used the cigarette packet or two pence piece again. I no longer had any need for the Ouija board. Behind my consciousness, thoughts, deeper than my voice, quieter than me, had emerged. It wasn't a voice in and of itself, or a being I could have a conversation with. I couldn't take it for coffee and discuss the deeper questions of life. It was more a sense. An idea. A guide. A broken dialogue, a catalogue of 'yes' and 'no's. It was the place I could go to find out where my friends were.

'Is Rob in the shop?'

The reply would come, instantaneously, assertively. Following, I'd find Rob.

It's the place I'd go to know whether the timing was right to steal wine. Was I unseen, unnoticed? And I'd move on the advice I received.

It was the place I'd go in the non-school days that followed; the hazy days with nothing to do except hang about in the woods, bottle of wine in one hand, spliff in another.

'Someone's coming.' We'd know. Hide our illegalities. And a man with a lead would walk by, whistling his dog. Coast clear we'd get the wine, the weed, from its hiding place, brushing off the moss and bits of twig.

Listening to the spirits became the guiding force to the everyday matters of my otherwise mundane existence. It was how I found myself, with Rob and Michael, one Thursday evening at a place I thought I'd never go.

*   *   *   *

Raising the thick-rimmed, scratchy plastic to my mouth, I shouted. Booming and echoing, my voice, I hoped, was intimidating as it cut through the chilly evening air. From behind and beside, the ammunition flew, small pellets hitting targets, pinging back and dropping to the floor. Shouting, laughing, destroying, we were indestructible.

And then the door swung open. Amid the stones Rob and Michael were throwing, and my bellowing through the traffic cone, a man emerged. It was getting dark but in the gloom it struck me that he looked like everything I expected of a Christian, as the door to the church youth centre swung shut behind him, protecting the innocence within; the youngsters we were frightening with our raucousness. But there was calm authority.

'Hi lads, can I help you?' His kindness was an open door, an invitation.

'What's the matter church man? We scaring the kids?'

After a quick succession of taunts, determined to intimidate, I resumed the traffic cone jeering.

Our teenage brutality, volatile and quick-to-anger attitude seemed to be defused by the guy's inability to react unreasonably. Somehow, in the space between our aggressiveness and the church man's quiet demeanour, a reasonable conversation began.

The lights flickered over Woking as we sat on a bench in front of the church. I could feel myself calming down, somehow being taken out of myself. The man introduced himself as Steve. Something in me liked Steve, enjoyed the attention, and wanted to talk. He told us of the youth club he ran behind the closed door – the Pathfinder Club, held every Tuesday as part of the work the church were doing in the area.

We weren't aware that they were at least two years younger than us; we just wanted to be there. Our boisterous young teen presence at the Pathfinder Club a week later unnerved some. It wasn't really the pool table or tuck shop that drew us, but the attention. We craved, we coveted the questions, the looks, the banter, the encouragements to join in, to take part. 'Hi, lads, I'm John.' Hand outstretched, more reserved than Steve, another youth leader introduced himself. I had been intrigued by John's talk at the club that evening. He spoke of a Spirit called the 'Holy Spirit' which was God himself. Making connections, we told him of the spirits locked within us, their guidance, goodness, and our cooperation.

'If they're not the Holy Spirit they won't help you, they'll only harm you.' John's assertion that any spirit that was not the Holy Spirit was bad; it confused me. I had experienced nothing but good things up to that point, enjoying their presence, their guiding, their assurances of company and safety.

*　*　*　*

I remember shafts of coloured light streaming through the stained glass, landing on the invited congregation. The lady with the feathers in her hair, adorned with orangey reds; black-suited men transformed by radiant blues; little girls with hair scraped into ponytails, best frocks already crumpled, aglow with yellows. Humid outside, the church felt shady, pews and floor cool to the touch, but there was a tightness of anticipation in the air. A few people dabbed their eyes with tissues. My mum sniffed into my dad's shoulder, gripping my hand tightly. Down the aisle, my granddad was in a box. Lid open, bedecked with flowers. Along with a procession of mourners, I made my way towards the coffin. Stuffing my hand into my pocket, I drew out a gift for my granddad. I stopped, not daring to look, not knowing what I might see. I threw my granddad's favourite chocolate bar into the casket and sat back down. The vicar raised his hands and uttered a few words heavenwards, barely recognized by the myriad of black-suited spectators. At 7 years of age, his was my earliest and least complicated experience of prayer.

That Thursday, seven years on, prayer felt very different. Steve placed his hand on my shoulder and said a number of things I wasn't sure I understood. And then, a word. A name. We'd been talking of the spirits, Michael, Rob and I, sharing stories with pride, keen to tell of our experiences – things we were excited and intrigued by; things that made us feel grown up; the way we could tap into knowledge about the future and gain guidance and direction. However, over those two weeks, the conversation had stepped up beyond our boasting. Steve had challenged, interjected, sharing his concerns and fears, placing doubt over our certainty that these were life-enhancing spirits. He had offered to pray for us.

With that name every muscle in me stiffened; there was a jolt of animosity, or fear; I wasn't sure. But I was struck by the overwhelming feeling that comes at the mention of someone you hate. Unmistakably physical, the name of Jesus had a power that disagreed with me. I jerked forwards, off the pew I had been sitting on, landing on the floor of the church with a thud. Coming to, embarrassed, I sat back up. The prayer continued, words and ideas washing over me, though none were as remarkable as the name that had come before. Prayer over, the evening continued in its usual way, pool and banter.

'How about coming to church on Sunday, lads?' asked Steve, as he locked the door behind us. Aside from my granddad's funeral, church had only been weddings, and Sunday school – once. That had been enough to know I didn't like it. I wasn't sure church was for me, if I would like it any better than I had then.

'Yeah, not sure, Steve. Maybe we'll see you here again next Thursday?' But something within me told me I should give it a go.

'Good morning. Welcome, lads.' Smiling broadly, an elderly man shook our hands at the door, handing us flimsy pieces of paper covered in news of the parish, who was on the flower rota, when the next church meal was, who had died.

'Where do we go?' I asked. Having shuffled into St John's the Sunday after Steve's invitation, Rob, Michael and I weren't entirely sure why we were there, least of all what we were to do.

He indicated the way. Down the corridor, into the main hall, with its carpeted floors and bright, cheerful posters; the

ancient juxtaposed with the modern, in an attempt to famil-
iarize the work of the past. We headed straight for the pew on
the right, furthest from the front; somewhere we could hide,
not be noticed or looked at.

We nudged and giggled our way through the next hour.
With the sounding of the last note of the final hymn, Steve
headed in our direction, unable to contain his enthusiasm.

'Good to see you, boys.' Steve indicated towards the front.
'What did you think?' 'It was all right.' I wasn't sure Michael
and Rob had any more idea of what to think than I had.
Mostly we had been bored. Bored but held in place on wildly
uncomfortable wooden seats, confused by a collection of
unpronounceable words, and intrigued as to the fervour at
which songs with simplistic tunes were sung. Mostly, it had
passed in a blur of our uninterested disengagement.

'Great, I want to introduce you to some people.' Leading
us to the front, Steve beckoned to a number of others, catching eyes, drawing them out of their earnest conversations.
Surrounded by five or six friendly faces, we were introduced.

'We'd really like to pray for you again. Would that be OK?'

All the interest struck me as bizarre, but it was kind and,
enjoying the attention, I was happy for anything to prolong
that. Lured into a sense of security by big sprays of flowers on
the stage, gentle piano music still being played, and children
running in and out of the doors, nothing could have prepared
us for what followed.

Rob was hunched over a washing-up bowl, heaving,
coughing, groaning, as his breakfast poured from between his
teeth. Hands were on his shoulders, comforting, controlling.
The sickness was propelling them to further intensity as they

prayed for the spirits to release Rob, to leave in the name of Jesus; their focus was removed from the vomiting, and raised to higher places as they evoked good, condemning evil.

The rapid filling of Rob's washing-up bowl barely registered as his face started to contort deliriously. He was the first to be prayed for, Michael and I perching on a pew, watching, waiting. Rob collapsed onto the floor, his body squirming in all directions. His hands were gripped into tight fists, smashing the ground, wildly thrashing into the air. Features on his otherwise placid face shifted into angry shapes, a snarl, a pinched mouth, eyes wide and fierce. And the noises, the sounds, the words that poured from Rob's mouth, so deep in their obscenity; Rob was an unrecognizable ball of rage, gripped by a force beyond anything I'd experienced. Meanwhile, the prayers continued, rhythmic, impenetrable. They persevered through the verbal and physical abuse, all the while proclaiming the name of Jesus over my friend.

The wave of mania ebbed away and the prayers grew quieter, matching Rob's calming down.

'Rob, you OK, mate? That was weird. You were going crazy.'

Wiping his mouth on his sleeve and standing to his feet, Rob no longer bore any resemblance to the writhing soul that we'd witnessed. He also had no recollection of the brute that had seized him.

'I just feel wiped out. Budge over, let me sit down.' And with that, Michael and Rob swapped places.

Watching Michael being prayed for wasn't any less frightening, even though at first his behaviour was vaguely amusing. His voice was high-pitched and squealing, like a child playing with helium balloons at a party. But just as soon as a personality of comedic value started to come through, it changed. Michael was absorbed into something that seemed more snide and manipulative. It bore a remarkable resemblance to the experiences we'd had with the Ouija board. One minute a spirit would be there – gentle, considerate – the next, someone else had taken over with anger or manipulation. Not just forces, definite personalities. The thing that was really obvious was the complete takeover as everything changed about my friends while they were prayed for. Then it was my turn.

Whole chunks of time were lost, like being caught in a deep sleep, as I was prayed for.

'You looked totally different.' Prayers over, Michael and Rob were quick to inform me of the shapes I'd created with my body, the contortions of my face.

'The stuff that came out of your mouth, George!'

The only reminders of the 'deliverance' I had were the bruises, purple and angry, emitting pain when I rolled over in bed for the next couple of days. Far from a cure, prayer seemed to empower something within us. There was a grip, tightening and strengthening, that took us from 'play', engaging to suit our childish desires, to something that existed beyond the realm of our control.

The battle with whatever our boyish ambitions had involved us in had only just begun.

Chapter 7

Not Me

Scents of jasmine, freshly cut grass and ice cream lay heavily on the air as the sun slowly, reluctantly, made its way behind the trees. The lazy onset of summer darkness created hours of relaxed park-time. The buzz of carnival, the excited screech of children at the arrival of the ice-cream van, and myriads of upturned faces; red-streaked backs where suntan lotion had not been applied properly, and umbrellas stowed away in picnic baskets 'just in case'. The park was crowded during the summer months, but we still felt it belonged to us.

We resumed our normal position – the doorway of the clubhouse now locked, public toilets standing behind. Beers were passed around, spliffs rolled. Nothing out of the ordinary for a Saturday night with a few mates from school.

I don't remember much of what happened next. I remember a growing tightness in my stomach. I remember heat, a pounding in my head. I felt I might explode. They told me later about how they had to pin me down, a friend on each limb. Like a madman I lashed out at them, requiring the force of four to force me to the ground, keeping them from harm. They told me how I changed, became unrecognizable.

'You suddenly got really strong.'

'It took four of us to keep you still.'

'I even had to hold your head!'

'Why were you trying to attack us?' A question I couldn't answer. I had no idea where the sudden rage had come from. I had no clue as to why I would want to try to attack my friends. I could barely even remember it. But I knew I had frightened them, and it wasn't the first time. Superhuman strength, strange voices and physical violence are not conducive to normal friendships. They didn't back off but, in the following weeks, I could feel their wariness.

It wasn't just me. Since being prayed for, Michael and Rob were also finding the spirits clamouring for more attention.

I remember running. I couldn't stop running. Leaping over pews, I recall being chased, hands grabbing at me, trying to stop me. But all I had was an uncontrollable urge to run. I was told to run. They told me to keep going, to not stop. Round and round and round. Climbing onto one pew, I reached out for the second, hovering somewhere between the two; knees on one, hands on the other as people clamoured for me. The tiled floor below beckoned me to fall, to place a foot down, to head for safety, and all the while the voices urged me on, to keep running, jumping, clambering.

They told me later it was funny, all things considered. The chase caused the pray-ers amusement in the midst of their fear, their disconcertion. Marie, Jimmy and John could see the comical side of all we were going through, Michael, Rob and I and them; the prayers, desperately asking God to get rid of whatever it was that was causing so much craziness.

The spirits in us were strong in those days, able to forcibly remove from our presence those who came too close. Somewhere between pew and floor, running and climbing, they had got hold of me, but whatever was controlling me had forced them away, powerfully rejecting their advances to control me, pray for me; it shook them off me. And I was away again, sprinting round the room like a freed animal that's been caged for a year.

We ran, freed from their grip, towards the bell tower, all the while controlled by something else, someone else. I have snatches of memory, moments of lucidity, a similar feeling to being drunk; parts are there, parts are lost forever, when we were taken over completely. Many parts are blanks I have filled in as others have recounted tales; I have added the colours, the images, the smells, the sounds, when really I have acres of lost time, moments when I became someone else.

We scurried up the narrow steps to where the ropes hung, inviting ringers to learn their melodies, to call people to worship in ways that take years of practice. We jumped on those ropes, grappling, swinging, taken over as the noise bellowed out in a cacophony of dissonance. I've said I have memories of this, but in reality I just had rope burns and the stories I was told.

For some reason, I managed to have a girlfriend at this time. But I scared her; maybe it was the unpredictability, or the tantrums, the fights. I took her to church with me a few times, but that only heightened the fear; the things she saw, the things she witnessed. The distance between us was insurmountable as I tapped into, dwelt in and moved through a whole world she didn't have access to. Or, rather, I had something in me that she would never be able to understand or be part of. We didn't last long.

I watched as, writhing around, his white jumper getting grass-stained and mud-smeared, our friends tried to pin Michael down a week after the bell-ringing incident. Like wiggling worms, no sooner had an arm been captured, it fought its way loose, striking and punching whichever poor soul was in range. Sitting on a flailing limb seemed to be the only way to stop the violence. That explained the bruises I was getting used to receiving.

Unnervingly, like a rabid dog, froth oozed out of Michael's mouth. He started spitting the white wetness, causing our friends to jump back in disgust.

'Should we call an ambulance?' I was afraid he was having some kind of fit. The kind you could die from.

'You did the same thing, George. He'll be fine.' One of our school friends, slightly more level-headed than the rest, was no less alarmed by what he was witnessing the three of us doing.

In time, Michael stopped spitting white bubbles, his body morphing back to himself. We had a fag, drank a couple of beers and kicked a ball around before heading back home. I would still run up the lane at the back of the estate, more afraid of the looming shadows and boyhood fables of lingering murderers than anything real. Besides, the Christians had said that everything was going to be OK. That Jesus was in control. Out of the ordinary was still an exciting adventure, a theme park attraction. Nothing to be afraid of.

I was busting for the toilet by the time I swung the front door open.

'Hiya!' I called out in response to my mum's greeting. It was late, but she wouldn't sleep until she knew I was home, despite the fact I had stormed out the house that afternoon. We'd been arguing about the state of my bedroom. Who'd said what? I had no idea. I remembered shouting, swearing, grabbing my mum, pushing her into a filing cabinet. She'd grabbed my hair. I'd resolved it all by running out, slamming the front door behind me.

'I'm off to bed, then,' she called out. There wasn't a hint of the earlier spat in her voice.

'Night, Mum.' I slipped into the downstairs toilet.

'Smash the mirror. Hit it. Go on, George. Smash the mirror.'

That voice, the 'not me'. I was used to its presence. It was constant now. But along with the uncontrollable, violent outbursts, the voice was changing. Underpinned with deep darkness, it was no longer fun, exciting. Subtly, day by day, it was attempting to suck the hope from me.

'George, smash the mirror.' A command I couldn't resist. Accompanying the voice, a deep urge was growing within me to destroy the mirror, lovingly hung by my mum over the washbasin. I wanted to see it in a million tiny glittering pieces. Anger was bubbling; I hated that mirror, in all its perfect glassiness. I wanted to see it destroyed.

Creating a fist I drove my arm into it and rejoiced as I saw it splinter, spidery cracks emanating from the bull's-eye. A few pieces tinkled into the sink.

Enraged that large fragments still hung there, I struck again. This time I was the victor, the basin filling with hundreds of irregular shards of glass.

My hand, torn to shreds, dripped bold, bright red blood over the pure white tiles, my T-shirt. I squeezed, desperate for more blood as I knelt on the floor. Bending over like a street painter, I wrote in the blood: DIE.

*   *   *   *

The sleepy relaxation that normally accompanies summertime was far from me as the days were absorbed by the growing presence of the spirits. One let me know his name. 'Nepal' was determined to rid me of any of the truth I may have heard every Sunday as I'd giggle through a sermon, or thrash around on the floor as I was prayed for.

'God doesn't love you,' it would say. 'Jesus doesn't care about you.' I wouldn't know how to combat these thoughts, and with each utterance, anxiety deepened. Those were shifting days; where once I thought we were alone on the planet, certainty of a supernatural world, of 'others', grew.

The commands to lash out, hurt someone, punch something increased in frequency and intensity. At times I could control what I did, and at others the urge was overwhelming. My friends were frequently on the receiving end.

'Jesus Christ came in the flesh, died and rose again.'

As Steve shouted those words, I dropped to the floor like a pack of playing cards stacked in triangles and knocked slightly by a finger. Crumpled and in a heap, I couldn't recall the events, except that moments before, Steve had been praying for me alone in the church lounge, when I had been overwhelmed by hateful urges.

'Kill him, punch him. Go on, get your hands round his throat.' That's what I had heard – serious, confronting, and commanding me to kill the one man who had shown love and patience. Steve had been looking at the Bible with me, pointing out various things about Jesus and who he was.

'Punch him. Flatten his face.'

After this, I only know what I was told. Steve says I got up and started charging round the room. Finding the piano, I sat down and started playing, banging out discordant notes before leaping up and turning on Steve. Fear had gripped him as I launched myself at him. All I remember is the overwhelming desire to harm him. Steve called out. The power of Jesus' name brought a close to the confrontation.

But I was out of control; the desire to destroy, to let loose, always descended in waves over me. I would want to smash things in Steve's house; his television, the windows, anything. The closer we got to Jesus, the greater the need to destroy. The spirits in me were afraid of Jesus, afraid of the mention of the cross, and lashed out, causing me to destroy as a way of keeping me under control, a way of frightening me into submission.

Simultaneously we were beginning to be a spectacle, an attraction. Or at least the effects of the spirit world on us were.

'George, mate, you were levitating.'

Week by week as we were prayed for, friends would gather to watch, sometimes afraid, sometimes amused.

'Like, your actual legs and arms left the floor.'

'It was scary!'

I lapped up the attention, but I also despised it, sometimes the onslaught of friends' opinions making the anger and violence inside gather momentum. The times of launching at my friends in parks, lashing out, threatening and having to

be controlled were no longer occasional. They were common-
place, and those friends who were afraid began to keep their
distance.

My parents saw few of these outbursts, but the spirits didn't
exclude them completely.

'Your parents are going to die. I'm going to kill them.'

I would want to know how, where, why. I'd want to know
what I could do to stop it. I didn't want to lose them, but
I just didn't know what I could do about it. I'd head back
to the church and talk with Steve. All the while he would
reassure me that what I was hearing wasn't truth, and that
God was in control. But it felt like the demons – for that
is what they were – were in control. I'd thought of them as
benevolent dead people, but they weren't. I'd been deceived.
They were evil spirits; the type Jesus called 'unclean' and sent
out of people, in the Bible. The longer they were there, the
more it felt as if I was in their grip. They were telling me what
to do, where to go. It was no longer a sense of calling on them
for guidance; they were my guidance, my control centre; they
had my mind. Yet I don't think I was afraid. I had seen and
felt their fear at the name of Jesus, their need to submit to
him. So I wasn't afraid, but I was in turmoil.

But then, all of a sudden, I was afraid. It was the day I
found myself on the railway tracks.

It was an ordinary day, hanging out with my mates; an
ordinary game of dare to run over the tracks. But I hadn't run.
I'd stopped, responding to an overwhelming urge to lie down,
spread myself across the line, like a man desperate for the end.

The vibrations were getting stronger, faster. My brain
rattled, my limbs beginning to take up the rhythms beneath

me. My friends were shouting, screaming, swinging between thinking I was messing around and being serious.

I tried to move my arms. I wanted them to lever me upright. But they wouldn't obey my commands. Neither would my legs. I could no longer even lift my head.

Heart-pounding panic seized me. For the first time since we had asked the spirits to come into us I was genuinely terrified. I was paralysed and the 14:20 to London was fast approaching.

In that moment I could see the newspaper headlines: 'Teenage boy killed by train'; 'Local boy dies on rail track'. I could see the photo of my grieving parents, a head shot of my most recent school picture, and the glib comments from my teachers painting me as better behaved and kinder than we all knew I was.

I gasped for air, desperately seeking it to fill my lungs. My chest was refusing to lift or lower, and my mouth was dry. My entire torso constricted as waves of nausea washed over me, and I shuddered along with the tracks, faster than the tracks. I fought with whatever was pinning me there, screaming at my muscles to move, pleading with my joints to bend, to rotate. It was futile. Everything faded but for the deafening roar of the train. I closed my eyes, waited for impact.

Then something grabbed me, gripping me round the neck, propelling me upwards. Somehow I stumbled from the tracks. On my feet, gathering winds caught my hair, my clothes, threatening to topple me over as the 14:20 roared by. An enormous clatter of metal, streams of blurred colours, lines of oblivious humanity mingled with 75 m.p.h. of commuter transport. I gasped for breath, fixed, not daring to move, staring across the tracks where the train had been, where I could have been. Everything over in an instant.

'George! George, what was that?'

'Are you mad?'

I honestly couldn't answer my friends' questions as they shouted from the bridge. I had no idea what had happened. And I *was* scared I was going mad.

'George, get off the tracks!'

I scrambled back up the embankment, thorns and twigs jabbing at my legs, tearing at my jeans, my hands scraping mud under my nails. I had to get away as fast as I could. Up, over the barrier, back to my mates. They were as pale as I felt. I slumped onto the concrete, relieved and very afraid. I think Rob handed me a fag.

I was filled with confusion. I knew that something awful had pinned me to those tracks, and that something beyond myself had pulled me up, rescuing me. I glanced at my hand, holding the cigarette; a small red blister was appearing on my index finger – an electric burn. I couldn't understand why that was the only evidence of the powerful surges that must have been travelling through those lines. Why wasn't I electrocuted – a miracle? Yet with every passing minute, doubt crept in. Did that really happen? Too surreal for reality, did I just imagine it?

Chapter 8

Peace Found and Lost Again

'You're going to die, George. You're going to die.'

Stronger and with greater clarity, over the next couple of days, the voice of this spirit refused to be quiet. And now it was plausible. I had seen and experienced the possibility of death. Being laid out on railway tracks, unable to move, focused the reality of the spirit's power; nothing else could account for what had happened. Nothing could explain my inability to move, and my friends had witnessed it. There was also no explanation for the way I was suddenly pulled free. Increasing in fear, I was aware that I no longer had control over what I said or did. In fact, I began to realize any sense of control I'd previously had was an illusion. Being under another authority, I felt disconnected, rootless.

'You're not going to live much longer. You're going to die.'

Lying in bed two days later, desperate for sleep to overtake me, the spirit intruded with every breath, filling my mind with its words, its deceit. I rolled over, shifting my body, in the hope it would eradicate the words from my mind.

'God hates you. Everybody hates you.'

I shuddered. Was it true? Did God hate me? Was he going to kill me and send me away from him forever? Was I going to hell? Was I going to die, and how could I be safe? Would I ever feel safe again?

'You're going to die.' I tried banging my head with my hands. I tried rolling on the floor. Then I hid under the covers. I was shaking, sweating, terror totally overwhelming me. Why wouldn't it stop?

'Shut up!'

Why had the spirit got more power over me than I had over it? Why couldn't I get it to obey me, to be quiet, to leave?

'Go away. Please go away.' Tears flowed as I begged, pleading to be free of the all-consuming fear and control.

'You're going to die. I'm going to kill you.'

As the anxiety and fear enveloped me, I became oblivious to everything but desperation to be rid of the spirit. I picked up my jacket and threw myself into it. Grabbing my keys, I stumbled down the stairs and out the door.

I zipped my jacket to my neck; the air was chilly, despite the fact that it was early summer. Walking quickly, every step filled with anxiety, I traced the way through my estate, each street named after a bird. Irrelevant and unimportant. Yet for that moment, I would have given anything to fly away. To be released from fear, from being trapped and oppressed.

I hit Steve's door, rapping my knuckles on the varnished wood until I was sure he'd hear, sure I'd woken him from sleep. I shouted for him, calling out, desperate.

'George?' The door had flown open to reveal a rather vague Steve. I really didn't care what he thought of me at that moment. I knew he was the only one who could help.

'Come in. What's up?' As I fell into his living room, I broke down. Tears cascading, body shaking, I expressed my terror at all that had happened on the railway tracks and all that had filled my mind since.

'George, do you believe that God made the world and that Jesus, his Son, is in control of everything?'

I nodded. I understood this much. From the Sundays I had spent at church, seeing my friends prayed for, and the violent response of the demons at the mention of Jesus' name, I had gathered that Jesus was bigger than demons and somehow more powerful. But I hadn't understood much beyond this.

'In order to be free from these spirits, you need to ask Jesus to be in control of your life, rather than the spirits,' Steve continued. He explained to me that only Jesus had power over everything, and just as the evil spirits were inside of me, so the Spirit of God, who was true and good, could come and take over; that he would set me free, rather than keep me imprisoned, as these spirits were doing.

Eyes closed, hands clasped in a way I'd seen many at church do, I prayed, asking God to help me. Nothing more than that. There was nothing else I understood at that point, only that God was powerful enough to rid me of the terror and whatever had seized me. My mind went quiet and something in me lifted. I waited for the evil voice to speak. It didn't.

Closing Steve's door behind me and heading into the starless night, I realized that the fear had ebbed away, leaving a soft sense of calm in its place. A mind that had been so full of terror and busyness felt empty and undisturbed. I could breathe the fresh air again, see the moon, remember what it was to be at peace.

And I knew that Jesus had done it. It was slow, quiet and unremarkable. There was no shaking or frothing at the mouth, no violent expression of the spirits leaving or powerful experience of God, but he had heard my prayer for help in the midst of terrible panic. I was changed; the direction of my life was altered as he drove the spirit out and replaced it with his peace.

I slept soundly for the first time in weeks.

* * * *

'So, then, just as the train was coming, it was like someone grabbed me by my neck and lifted me up. I stood to the side of the tracks, just as the train whizzed by.'

I looked out across the sea of hundreds of faces. Faces filled with interest, disbelief, bemusement. I continued my story, explaining how I'd gone to Steve's and prayed for God to help me, for Jesus to be in control.

'If anyone wants to talk more, or ask questions, then come and find us at lunchtime. We're going to be in room C4.'

A few people clapped as we climbed off the stage, adrenalin powering our limbs. Along with Steve, Rob and I had managed to tell the whole of Year 10 about our experience with the spirit world.

C4 was filled with the sticky smell of summertime adolescence that lunchtime. We tried to answer questions, and we offered to pray for our peers.

There were an extra eighteen to twenty teenagers at the youth club that Thursday. To cater for the questions, Steve set up a new group. Week by week we'd open Bibles, learning about Jesus, who he was and what he'd done.

I carried on going to church. Intensity of praying decreased, attention on us became minimal, and it all became a little mundane. There was a big gap between what I'd experienced and what I understood. Content to know God was in control and I was free from fear, I didn't realize there might be more to being a Christian than just going to church.

I wasn't the only one losing interest. Captured by the excitement of my story, rather than a relationship with God, my school friends began to slowly slip away from church. Then I met Hannah.

A pokey little garden shed provided the sleepover venue for Hannah and her friend. Alex was a mate from school and he fancied Hannah, so I reasoned that trying my luck with her friend would be a sensible idea.

'Give us a leg up.' Alex stood, hands resting on the fence, face expectant. I cupped my hands beneath his feet, and he propelled his weight forwards, grabbing at the wood and heaving himself over. Being taller, I could get myself up and over, the only casualty being my thumb – a tiny wedge of dirty pine pinning itself under the skin; intolerable discomfort, but left to figure its own way out.

'They're in here,' Alex whispered as his hand gripped the rusty handle of the shed door. Pushing it open, the girls looked at us, wide-eyed, giggly, and confused.

'Hi, ladies. Can we come in?'

That night, Alex and I did a kind of swap; he chose her friend, and I lay down next to Hannah. I slept there, and the following day, Hannah became my girlfriend.

In my mind, I wanted to restrict the relationship physically to hand holding, kissing. By this point, the church had instilled some religious values in me; no sex before marriage, that kind of thing. My heart may have been cold towards Gód, but I still wanted to follow through those small murmurings of belief, however they might play themselves out in my life.

But, being a young lad, feeling passionate, in love with Hannah, I began to question God. Why was he trying to stop something natural? Why did God want to spoil all our fun? Kissing would turn to touching, touching would lead to guilt, saying sorry, feeling trapped; trapped by a conflicting set of desires, ambitions and intentions, all the while divorced from any sense of a relationship with God, actions flowing from what I thought was love.

Sex began to creep into my soul, stealing my thoughts, grabbing any attention I might have paid to God. It was fun, exciting, and it felt great. As I fell head over heels with Hannah, I all but terminated my relationship with God. I'd misunderstood who God was, what he'd done and what he wanted for me. I'd considered him a killjoy and his ways redundant in my teenage scramble for satisfaction.

*   *   *   *

My sister had a great collection of records. *True Blue* by Madonna, *Tango in the Night* by Fleetwood Mac. Stacked high, they were a tower of temptation. Lingering outside her room, eyes fixated, I was eager to get my fingers on those smooth sleeves; to whip out the floppy plastic, and gently place it on the turntable, then move the arm, lower it, and wait for the first dulcet note. A place to breathe, to connect. So I would wait until I could hear my sister deep in conversation downstairs, and then I would grab

whatever my heart desired from her room, and scurry back
to mine.

'Argh! George!' My sister would come flying through my
door, ignoring the 'Keep Out' sign. Launching herself on
me, we'd start clawing, screaming, shouting. It was only ever
resolved by the intervention of Mum.

Like a house of mirrors, these occurrences were reflected
throughout the familial relationships. Mum and Dad, Mum
and me; Harriet and me; inflicting damage verbally, physically. With my sister, we could put it down to sibling rivalry.
With Mum – my teenage angst. Dad and Mum? That was a
deeper and vastly more complicated tangle.

It was a tangle that my mum was determined to unravel.
Gathering strength from Al-Anon, a group for friends and
relatives of alcoholics, she began to realize she couldn't change
my dad; she couldn't stop the drinking; she couldn't fix him.

'I'm going to divorce your dad.'

No longer sharing the same bed, Mum had my sister and
I in her bedroom, telling us what we'd heard rumblings of
so many times before – threats of divorce, of ending it all,
of walking out and never coming back. But this was different. There was determination in her eyes, and her demeanour
was calm; sad but sure. Not thrown out in the heat of the
moment, or to inflict pain; just a clear statement of truth.
And she was telling us before she told him.

*   *   *   *

Dad and I stared sorrowfully out through the windscreen of
his Vauxhall Cavalier as rain lashed against the steamy glass.

'If I'd thought for one second my drinking would make your mum leave me,' he said, 'I would have given it up.'

A number of weeks had passed since Mum had made her decision, stuck by it, and they had started the process of selling the house, eradicating the lingering memories of happier times.

This was the most we talked about it. I wondered why, if there was even a 5 per cent chance of saving the marriage, my dad hadn't tried, pleaded for support. He'd promised me we'd talk about the break-up, as soon as Mum had broken the news to him. He'd told me he was leaving, telling me like I didn't know, like it was a decision between a married couple, sacred within their bond before children were involved; like somehow we were still protected from sides, a neutral factor in a far from neutral agreement. But he'd left that day and gone on a bender. Finding solace in the four walls of his local, there'd been no room for conversation. Annoyed with Mum for speaking to us before Dad, and feeling the absence of him as he drowned himself in all that alcohol had to offer, I felt isolated. With a myriad of feelings as complicated as any I'd felt before, I struggled to make sense of everything – and that included what the church told me. So I turned my attentions to Hannah.

And yet here we were, shivering with the cooling of the engine, my dad as broken as any man, uttering regret that had never had enough conviction behind it to actually do anything.

The summer I was 16 approached at speed, bringing with it GCSEs. Hannah and I had been together a long time, and with the choice of living arrangements placed before me, I couldn't bear to see Dad drifting off by himself. I feared for his health, for his loneliness and choice of companion, and I felt an allegiance. I chose to move in with him.

Establishing myself in his flat we were, once again, men together. I felt excited, free and grown up, and church had become a distant memory, lost in a haze of exams, sex and family politics.

*   *   *   *

I was never going to do it. Dad was never going to do it, either. So it piled up, a dirty, festering stack of bean-encrusted, takeaway debris on old crockery. The kitchen at Dad's flat was overrun with items of discarded tins and leftovers. It contrasted sharply with the rest of the flat, which felt like a sad, meagre demonstration of the loss of a marriage. We had a dining table and chairs, bare wood floors and a mountain of boxes that remained unpacked. Dad also had his chair.

Dad was dozing that day when Richard, a mate from college, where I was now doing a BTEC, dropped round with a few cans of beer.

'What you got there, mate?' I was intrigued by what else Richard seemed to be carrying.

'Want one?' Richard opened the bag, jiggling it under my nose.

'What are they?'

'Speed, mate. Try it.'

Speed was horrendous. But having tried most things as a young teenager, it was new, it was more grown up. It signified a new era.

We did half a gram that first time. And it got us walking. We left the flat that evening and didn't come back until morning. Walking, walking, and talking.

'Mate, you were great at school.'

'Yeah, mate, so were you.'

'Life's so weird, isn't it, mate?'

'Yeah, mate.'

Incessant conversations of nothingness that felt deep and profound while we chewed away on gum, words scattered through minty saliva, teeth clashing, chattering . . .

'So, mate, I've been thinking. The way I see it . . .'And off we'd go again, in a discussion of something pitiful and empty.

'Mate, that's so profound. '

'Got more gum?'

All night, we must have walked miles.

* * * *

'I'm not feeling anything. Can you feel anything, Rich? 'I was disappointed with the lack of high as the train coursed its way to Guildford, our destination for the evening, to a popular nightclub.

'Nah, mate, not yet.'

'Oh . . . 'And then it hit. I glanced at Rich, at my other friends. Eyes like saucers, blinking, staring. Boom! And the chewing, the chatting, the continual movement, noise. An inability to keep still, to be quiet. Getting to the club at 9:30 p.m., we'd dance until it closed at 2 a.m.

'Yeah, go George!' I clambered on the podium, dancing, jumping, moving to the beat of the music, the speed-induced beat in my head that got me, thrilled me, took hold of me. I couldn't stop. In that moment, dancing was all I had, all I wanted. In reality, I actually hated dancing.

'Got any Bonjela?' Groaning in pain was usual after a night on speed. My mouth would be full of ulcers, oozing and open like craters on the surface of the moon. Having a mouth on fire, yet tasting and smelling rancid, the need to brush, to eat or drink was crucial yet impossible. The only relief that could vaguely suppress the pain would be some soothing gel.

'Mate, shut up, would you?'

I'd usually be at Richard's on those mornings after. His dad had died when he was young and his mum, unable to control Richard, wouldn't interfere. She was gentle, nice, but totally unable to exert any authority. Richard couldn't bear my voice in the mornings. I couldn't bear his, or anyone else's we'd been with, for that matter. Their voices reverberated, grated in my head. They'd been there all night; a constant chattering, gnawing away through my ears and into my skull, which was sleep-deprived, dehydrated and overstimulated. Exhausted, the desire would be for silence. Days were wasted like this, waiting for the come-down to subside, the aching muscles, the ulcerated mouths. We'd watch the TV but be too tired to focus, eyes too awake and scratchy to sleep. Just as normality resumed, we'd start all over again the following weekend.

And what about God? God was far away now. Truthfully, I just didn't think about him any more.

Chapter 9

A Dark Treadmill

I admired my neatly ordered drawer. A wrap of speed and weed were lined up side by side. Regimented, small parcels of my growing business. I enjoyed the way they looked, the organization of all I was achieving, who I was becoming.

When the weekend started, the feeling of a little packet in your pocket was exciting. It was your doorway, your entrance to a good weekend. It beckoned and tempted, dancing in your pocket; it was like the simmering of a really good dinner on the stove. You wanted to dig in and sample. But you wouldn't want to spoil your appetite, so you'd wait, anticipation mounting until it was time.

You'd open the wrap – a folded magazine or newspaper – carefully, like an envelope, taking care not to lose a single particle. And then you'd lick the paper, just to make sure every little scrap had been savoured, used. If it was good stuff it would make your tongue tingle. Excitement edged to every part of your body. That was how I knew I could make money from it; that was how it had started.

Next to the packets of weed and speed were some notes and a few scattered condoms; the tell-tale signs of my ongoing relationship with Hannah. On speed, the need for sex increases, always wanting more. The boldness of my drawer, symbolizing all I'd become, was foolish; no attempt to hide things, no fear. In those days I was brash and confident. Having left school days behind, living with my dad, and a BTEC in business at college underway, I thought I was in control.

My clunky mobile phone rang. Shrilly, demanding attention, yet brick-like, it required effort to pick it up. It was one of those come-down days. My body ached and my eyes were bleary, making concentration difficult.

'Yeah?'

Someone wanted some speed that afternoon. The desire to make some quick cash enlivened my thick, furry joints, and I stirred myself from the dozy daydreams I'd been having.

'Just going out, Dad.'

'Yeah,' Dad grunted from his armchair as I barely popped my head round the door. Some days I wouldn't even see his face; the discomfort of his isolation and his physical and emotional decline got to me too much. Easier to look away.

My backpack was slung over my shoulder as I manoeuvred my bike from where it was propped in the entrance to the flat, and went down into the bright sunshine. Blinking, I hopped on and willed my aching legs to pedal.

You wouldn't always know the people you delivered to, but you'd take their money, and over time, faces became familiar. Regular customers. The cuts I gave them were fair, but you'd always sell for higher than you bought. You could get twice the amount of money you bought it for. And you could keep a fair amount for yourself. Quick, easy, minimal risk as I'd glance around, pass it on, grab the money, pedal away. Every intention of the delivery would be to look as normal as possible; mates meeting, or people bumping into each other. Nothing out of the ordinary. Making money and getting high were a big enough payout for the risk. Somehow I managed to make it work.

I'd pedal home, sling my bag back on the door peg, making sure my textbooks and folders were back inside ready for the next day's classes at college. If I went.

That was the problem with college, really. I didn't go all that often. I was getting further behind, as the majority of Monday was hit and miss as to whether the weekend's antics had worn off enough to crawl out of bed, or to focus. I was missing deadlines. And then I discovered ecstasy.

My mate's house was our party house, a haven of hedonism and escape. With divorced parents who weren't around much, and older siblings, drugs flowed easily and freely, as did company of all ages and backgrounds. It was a place that made new experiences accessible and acceptable, a place to go to be free, and lose yourself in whatever had been newly discovered.

Someone handed me half a pill, and I immediately took it. I'd learned not to ask questions, preferring the risk, the experience. Sinking back against the wall of the living room, I settled into feelings of calm; a peace that was indescribable, a euphoric sense of love for all those around me. I loved them all. They all amazed me, made me feel happy, welcome, my family.

'I love you, mate. I love you. I really do.' I think I went round the whole room, declaring love, telling everyone how wonderful they were, before slipping out of the front door and walking into the night.

I found myself at the lake, headphones jammed into my ears, lyrics floating and mingling with my own thoughts, confronting, calming, encouraging, telling me what to think about myself, my world. The lake lay calm and still in a haze of blue softness as the darkness started to lift; shades of night colliding with the start of a new day. Birds were beginning to announce the arrival of dawn, greeting the sun long before it became visible. I sat there watching as more detail etched its way into the world, the light highlighting, showing the beauty of where I'd found myself. The lyrical music gave way to house, trance, something more 'my thing'. The beat and the birdsong together were like a symphonic orchestra especially arranged for me; a light and sound spectacle, an injection of love and euphoria. Every part of me felt alive – falsely, chemically, alive.

By the time the sun had driven itself fully into the sky and I was back at my mate's house, sitting in the garden, propped up by the garden fence, I was aware I was feeling too hot. Prickly hot, hot from the inside, not just 'too many clothes on' hot. My arms, my legs, my face irritated me. Scratching away, I wanted to pull the skin off, sheet by sheet, in a bid to cool myself, relieve myself of the itch and heat.

'I don't feel so good,' I told my friend.

'You don't look it.'

The joking tone of his voice made me panic even more. I felt alone, isolated, afraid of whatever it was that was making me feel this way. Scared the ecstasy was messing with me, I was anxious. I needed help.

'I'm gonna go home.'

'See ya later, George.'

I started the journey home, stumbling. My head hurt, I could see blotches on my fingers. Big, fat, red blotches. My breathing was heavy and laboured. I couldn't catch my breath.

'Dad, I really don't feel good.' I edged my way to the sofa. Dad got me a duvet and I sat there itching and fretting for most of the weekend. The redness and blotchiness didn't go away, but I didn't die – as I feared I might.

The anxiety of what I had done to myself that Saturday night stayed with me until Monday when I decided I'd had enough of feeling ill and scared, and should see a doctor.

'Hmmm, yes, I see. I think you have scarlatina.'

'What's that?'

'Scarlatina . . . scarlet fever.'

For now I was relieved. I must have caught it from someone at the party. It was always like that, though, taking drugs. When you took a pill, snorted coke, inhaled an aerosol, you never really knew what was in it, how you'd react. In the back of your mind was always the 'what if?' question. For the sake of bravado and excitement you'd ignore it, suppress it, but sometimes it reared its ugly head, catching you unawares. However, at that stage I was still too interested in drowning out the noise of life, of my daily concerns, my sense of futility and meaninglessness, to take any note of the warning. My days of church and God were also becoming hazy memories.

*   *   *   *

The rhubarb and custards were good. The wall I was sitting on felt hard and knobbly under my backside, but the rhubarb and custards were sweet and sugary, and the music in my ears lulled me into a sleepy trance. I didn't care that my teeth were grinding and my face was pinched and screwed up like a bulldog's. The yellowy pinkness of the sweets and the rhythm in my head placated me. I enjoyed the way ecstasy did this to me, took me off on my own, enjoying the peace and quiet. A world where only I existed, save for nature which sat beside me as company, with music providing our soundtrack. I needed that at that moment. Towards the end of my first year at college, amidst all the turmoil at home, less than perfection in my relationship with Hannah, I was also failing my BTEC.

'You need to sort things out,' my head of year had said. 'Your work isn't up to scratch.' I'd promised to try.

Then Hannah and I broke up.

'I just don't love you any more,' she told me.

In the woods, I'd tried to speak, tried to tell her how I felt, but she was adamant. A few weeks later she slept with Rob. All the while I had wanted her to be my bride.

I didn't really know what to do about that, except sit on that wall sucking on rhubarb and custards, high on ecstasy. I'd loved her. I missed her. Singleness hurt in a way it hadn't before. At the come-down of every high, people would be in couples. In the clubs, at my mates' houses, everywhere I went, screaming at me of love, of the thrill and anticipation of sex, of lust, of everything I had had and lost. The drugs intensified those feelings. I turned to porn in an attempt to grasp at something; something to satisfy my cravings, to fill the longing, the emptiness, the hole Hannah had filled. It was empty, though. There wasn't any satisfaction, there wasn't any love. Like the drugs, the more you used, the more you wanted. I became desensitized to it all, only serving to increase the isolation and loneliness.

And the promise to my head of year was empty. After that conversation, I didn't go back. With a handful of GCSEs, but no other qualifications, I was aimless and directionless.

* * * *

Mark decanted beer from tins he'd pulled from his bag, into our empty coke bottles.

'Here ya go, lads. This will see us through the afternoon.'

Having already spent our lunch break knocking back pints in the pub, another beer wasn't going to make a lot of difference.

'Cheers, mate. I suppose we'd better head back.'

It took every effort to drag our inebriated bodies back to the office for an alcohol-fuelled afternoon of tele-canvasing.

I couldn't hang around the flat long; Dad's drinking depressed me and I needed to earn some money. Just before we broke up, Hannah had suggested a job with a home improvements firm. I decided to go for it, finding I was good at sales and enjoyed the banter with the lads. While I liked chatting to customers on the phone, the work was monotonous.

Prank phone calls to fellow colleagues were high on the list of ways to get through the morning. These sorts of jokes passed the time quite adequately, but mostly we just looked forward to lunchtime, when we'd grab our coats and speed off to the pub.

The pints were a pound each, elevating the desire to cram in as many as possible before our hour was up; four was the average. Then, with coke bottles stashed away in bags, we'd decant another pint each carefully through the narrow top, spending the afternoon drinking beer disguised as Coca-Cola.

I worked with one of my old school pals. Having been promoted to team leader for the area, I would slip him a few extra shifts in his wages and he would slip me a few extra beers at lunchtime. A winning combination.

* * * *

The club was stacked wall to wall with bodies oozing with sweat and anticipation. Heads nodding, arms swinging, hips gyrating. Pulsing to the beats emanating from the turntables, the speakers. Drum and bass reverberated deep inside your chest, to the ends of your fingers, until your whole body was taken over, controlled, forced into heavyweight movement in tune, in time, in line. Based in Victoria, this was a nightclub Mark had introduced us to. Mark was a breath of fresh air to me; a face outside of Woking, someone new, with excitement to offer.

It was Friday night, and we were letting off steam after a cooped-up week selling windows. Away from the bar, in a darkened corner, Mark reached into his inside pocket, a small bag, white powder and a credit card in his hand. He indicated, 'Do you want some?' Flicking a little onto the card, white and dusty, hanging on the corner, he pressed his index finger to his nose, and sniffed deeply.

'Sure.' I'd been experimenting with speed but I'd been finding the comedown awful; more depressing than reality, without the highs. They didn't call speed 'poor man's coke' for no reason. So an offer of the good stuff was hard to refuse.

It was like treacle heading down the back of your nose, hitting the throat, followed by a bitter taste. Count the seconds . . . thirty . . . then an impact of confidence, of happiness. You're more 'together' than when you're on speed; more in control. Everyone is a friend and the dance floor beckons.

A few hours later, I was turning the key in the front door of the house I shared with Dad in Walton Road. The TV was on, the newsreader beginning to wake the world up with whatever sadness had happened overnight. Behind the curtains, the sun was beginning to eke its way out from the darkened horizon. Dad sat in the shadows, slumped in his armchair. No movement, no attempt to go to bed; cans of Special Brew, scattered around his feet, had been his night's entertainment. Now he had slipped into an unconscious slumber as the day began to confront us with its responsibilities.

Walking by, pushing open my bedroom door and falling into bed, I mentally calculated the shots I'd had, and thought about water. My stomach grumbled, chewing itself; I wasn't sure when I had last eaten. I groaned at the thought that there was only Special Brew in the fridge. Sleep was the way out of the creeping depression which threatened to overpower me. I felt a vague sense of frustration at Dad's irresponsibility before I shut my eyes. The irony of this thought completely passed me by.

A dark treadmill of alcohol, cocaine, a number of jobs, an attempt at A-levels, and trying to get over Hannah filled the next two years.

I dragged myself into a new job in an IT company. With the majority of the workforce under 25, the vibe was young, vibrant and cocaine-fuelled.

'Come on, guys, quickly.' Jeremy whipped the lines of coke out as we gathered round. I noticed the mid-morning remnants of pastries and coffee stains on the huge table where we scored our fix. Coffee break cocaine in the boardroom.

'Matt's coming. Quickly!' Our boss was returning, making his way down the corridor, ready to start the next meeting. Giggling, wiping the remnants of white powder off the table, we took our places, ready to begin, as high as kites. A cacophony of sniffs echoed around the room. Matt knew; he just turned a blind eye. The work got done and I had already been promoted to team leader. The cocaine was simply our coffee.

We hung out a lot at Jeremy's home. Then one time, I looked around me. Faces I'd grown accustomed to slumped in sofas, armchairs. Some smoking, some snorting a line. Beers, a few crisps. On a side table, family photos; Jeremy as a smartly dressed 6-year-old; as a teenager, spotty and nonchalant.

'I love you, George.' Squished into the sofa to my left, one of Jeremy's friends was filled with the stupidity of narcotics.

'Don't be an idiot. You don't love me.' The charm of the drugs scene was fading. I was becoming increasingly frustrated by false declarations, false people, false feelings. Like the drugs themselves, the high had lasted for a while, but it was fast losing its shine.

'I don't want to do this any more.' There was that thought again. I'd been dealing coke, selfishly cutting it with other things – talc and sugar – then selling, making loads of money. Even my closest mates wouldn't ever see a full gram of pure coke. But the promise that never delivered was turning into an irritation.

'I'll go to the pub, but I won't do any coke.' There was a small voice of discontent with a lifestyle that had dominated my every waking moment. But two beers later I was taking a line, sniffing deep, getting high. Ever telling myself today would be different, it never was. I was trapped. I wanted out.

Chapter 10

Thailand

Sinking back against the napkin-clad headrest, I closed my eyes. Below, the engines started to roar. My ears heard sweet papers rustling as travellers popped boiled sweets into drying mouths, simultaneously adjusting to the sensation of movement. A commanding voice requested attention over the Tannoy, reminding us of potential dangers, imminent emergencies. Only the few who found flying a frightening experience, who were convinced this life-saving information was most likely going to be necessary, took any real notice.

As the wheels left the runway, I swallowed, my ears popping and clearing as the words my dad had read to me last night reverberated through my mind:

> If you can talk with crowds and keep your virtue,
> Or walk with Kings - nor lose the common touch,
> if neither foes nor loving friends can hurt you,
> if all men count with you, but none too much;
> If you can fill the unforgiving minute
> With sixty seconds' worth of distance run,
> Yours is the Earth and everything that's in it,
> And – which is more – you'll be a Man my son!
>
> *(Rudyard Kipling, 1865–1936)*

I forced the tears back, recalling this rare father-son moment, reminiscent of those childhood days when the evenings drew to a close and alcohol promoted closeness. Having decided the problems in my life were Woking, my job, my home life and my friends, after three years working for the IT company, I had handed in my notice and bought a round-the-world ticket. I was 22.

Touching down in Thailand, wedged between my mates Greg and Sam (it was at their invitation I was here), I contemplated the adventures ahead. Convinced this was a new start, my plan for the year was to pursue contentment and happiness away from all the things that had dragged me down.

'Taxi? Taxi?' Men forced their faces into mine, touting their business. Bangkok airport was hectic and hot. It was heat I had not experienced before. It was engulfing, all-consuming, and had the immediate effect of gluing T-shirts to backs and hair to foreheads. The people swarmed, shoving, scurrying about on business, on holiday, backpackers . . . They churned up the heat as they moved, pushing it around, hot gusts that oppressed rather than relieved. Aside from a lads' week of booze and dancing in Tenerife and Ibiza, and family holidays in France, I'd not really been abroad. This was utterly disorientating, overwhelming, and I swung between feelings of panic and excitement.

Initially we headed for Khao San Road, a heady mix of cafés, bars and motels – a traveller's paradise, a Thailand created around Western hedonism. It was like being at home, but bathed in constant sunshine and oppressive heat. It was there I discovered I could walk up to people in a bar and strike up a conversation, one moment a stranger, the next a friend. At home I found relationships difficult without the aid of alcohol or drugs; people seemed locked in to their own space, inaccessible to me. Here, things were different.

I was adopted by two French guys who delighted in calling me 'Roast Beef' and spent the days in the bar playing pool and knocking back an insidious mix of strong vodka and fiery, spicy Thai Red Bull. Food was served to dull the continuous hangovers. With each passing day I bought more and more into the traveller lifestyle.

'Ten baht?'

'Fifteen.'

'OK, twelve.'

I haggled my way down to pennies for outrageous shorts and shirts; traveller-style and ridiculous. I thought I was cool, I could haggle like a local and yet dress like a foreigner, my clothes a neon sign pointing me out as a Brit who thought he belonged but didn't.

Writing home, I would tell my friends and family of my adventures across the world, imagining myself as some sort of undercover brigadier surveying new lands, sampling drinks, food and the Muay Thai boxing rings. I amused them and I amused myself. I thought I was king of the world.

With buoyed confidence, we headed to the north of Thailand, spending time in bars, with girls and on mopeds. We would spend hours driving around the roads, exploring villages and getting lost. Once, I struggled for four hours to find my way back to our motel in Chiang Mai, and for the first time I felt real panic and vulnerability; the tough guy act was a veneer, kept in place by the easy trappings of friends and tourism. On a moped in a jungle, I was alone – really alone. I eventually found my way home.

I signed up a few days later to experience the jungle properly, safely, but without Sam and Greg, joining up with another group of travellers for a three-day trek through the jungle; tents strapped to backs, riding elephants, swimming through waterfalls. I thought I was in paradise. I was interacting with people who liked me, wanted me around. In reality, a false sense of security and relationship was being created by the beauty of the world around us; it was all about shared experiences of adrenalin, and there being no one else to spend time with. But for now, it felt like all I'd been searching for; the trappings of home, of Woking, were left far behind. Like God was left far behind.

Some time afterwards, I was back with Sam and Greg. A 24-hour coach journey stretched ahead of us. Dozing through it seemed the best option, so we popped Valium pills into our mouths. Towns, villages and fields passed in a blur of exhausted passivity. Arriving in Bangkok, we got a hotel room for the three-hour stopover just so we could sleep. Eventually we arrived on the island of Koh Samui, to the south. White beaches, palm trees; more paradise. The intention was to stay here for a few weeks before heading over to Malaysia and onwards through Asia, to Australia.

* * * *

The stench was overwhelming; Parmesan cheese mixed with damp dog. Encouraged by the heat, Greg's trainers were causing a problem. Halfway to the solicitor's, we stopped the taxi, forcing our friend to throw his trainers from the window.

'Mate, you could have at least made an effort.'

'I ran out of time. Couldn't find anything.'

'Seriously though, on contract signing day.' Greg, dressed in an Arsenal shirt and a mismatched pair of shorts was now shoe-less; his legs were covered in scars from a myriad of moped accidents. About six months had passed since that first day in Bangkok airport, and we were putting down roots. We'd always intended to keep moving, seeing as much of the world as possible, but after an eight-day foray in Malaysia, I was desperate to get back to Koh Sumui.

'Guys, I don't think I actually want to carry on with you.' I had a year to travel, to see the world; Sam and Greg only had three months, and were determined to see as much as possible. Thailand hadn't grabbed them the way it had me.

'But George,' they'd said, 'Singapore will be amazing.'

'I'm missing Saichon, I'm missing the bar. I dunno, just everything felt right for me there.'

A week earlier we'd got on the minibus heading to our hotel in Malaysia. It was meant for eight people but there must have been at least twelve on board. It was cramped, smelly, hot, and I'd felt totally out of place for the first time since leaving England. Sadness overwhelmed me as I began to panic that I'd left behind the answer to my problems – Thailand and Saichon.

Saichon . . . Her hips moved rhythmically to the beats the DJ flipped out, each record seeming like it were made for her petite frame. Flashes of disco light glanced across her bare arms, refusing to rest on any part of her body; tantalizing, tempting me to move nearer. This was a regular haunt, a club located in the centre of Koh Sumui; the drinks were cheap, the drugs easy to get hold of, and the music was good. We spent a fair amount of time in the other bars around the island, but this one was the best for dancing. My confidence with the girls was growing, but it didn't come easy to me; not like it did for my friends.

'Hi, I'm George.' I had dared to make a move, willing myself to ask her name, to move closer, to act with confidence.

'Saichon.'

'That's a nice name. Can I buy you a drink, Saichon?'

That night, Saichon had come back to the bungalow we were living in, and it felt great. I actually thought I'd found the answer to life every day she was mine. And so, Malaysia felt wrong; everywhere else, anything else felt wrong.

'Have a great time in Singapore.' I had waved to my friends as the bus had pulled away, feeling no regrets. Seeking out the hotel we had first fallen for in Koh Sumui, I set up a happy reunion with Saichon. I was home.

Two days later, there was a knock on my door.

'Hi, George. Singapore wasn't for us.'

Sam and Greg, travel weary, were laden down with their bags.

'Pub?' We headed to our English home-from-home that night, our favourite bar – the only place you could get, at a price, English cider. Within a week I was working there, and within a few more, Darren, the owner, had offered to let us buy it.

We celebrated in the bar that night. The bar that was now in our names – having signed a contract that was all in Thai, and handed over £8,000. Saichon slipped her arms around my waist.

'Congratulations, George.' She handed me a Strongbow, an unusual choice of drink in Thailand. Running an English-style pub, Darren had been one of the first English guys we'd met on arrival in Koh Samui, and Strongbow had been a welcome break for me; a couple of weeks of drinking strong Thai beer had begun to make me unwell.

This was also where I had met pretty Thai Saichon. We communicated in broken English. Ferocious arguments, fuelled by drink, were always a heady reminder of the family I'd left behind.

I surveyed the room, taking it in; mine. Clean and fresh-smelling, air cooled by a fairly robust air-conditioning system; tables for around thirty people, an American-style pool table, a big screen. Newly acquired friends stood about, clinking glasses, rowdiness increasing with each opening of the fridge or draw on the tap. My girlfriend, tonight, was smiling sweetly up at me. I owned a bar on an island paradise. For that moment, my worries were left in England; I had bought contentment in Thailand.

* * * *

It was the busiest night we'd had. We had no special promotions or attractive lure. But on the queen's birthday, when every other bar in town was closed, our doors stayed open. In Thailand, royalty were just that: royalty. Elevated to the status of gods, most public places had framed photos of the king and queen – gold-rimmed, ornate spectacles of respect and worship placed above doorways, on mantelpieces; mini-shrines, inviting the royal family into your home as if they were your very own. Every place closed its doors to trade when a member of the family celebrated their birthday, by royal decree – except for us, on account of the fact that people still needed to eat, whether the queen was a year older or not.

Wall to wall, customers moved, pulsating to the strong beat of English-fused Thai, a strange concoction of cheaply filtered music. Sweat dripped, mingling with condensation, and cocktails flowed fast as everyone got excited by the party atmosphere of a crammed bar. I ran round like a headless chicken, trying to keep a lid on everything. Lining the bar, small brown jars slowly filled with cards and papers: scribbled 'IOUs', the way we kept tabs. Everyone would settle with us at two in the morning, the end of the night.

'Right, that's it everyone. Night's over.' I was shutting down the lights, flicking off the music, beginning the process of closing. 'Settle up, folks, time to leave.' There was a general murmur, the early signs of people fiddling in pockets, making their way to the bar, thinking of taxis, mopeds, heading home; the shine wearing off the party as soon as darkness descended and the speakers fell silent.

'*Leave! Leave! Leave!*' Screaming in Thai, two policemen had walked in, shouting at the customers, forcing and pushing them through the doors. I glanced at the clock; a little past 2:04 a.m. My customers fled the bar, not waiting to pay, as the policemen collected up the pots, pouring out the money, a full evening's takings sinking into the pockets of thieves.

'Owner? Who runs this place?'

I stepped forward.

'You're under arrest for opening past licensing hours.'

Most of this was in Thai, half English. I understood. I tried to argue, knowing it was futile.

'Follow us.' The irony of the Thai system meant that despite being well over the alcohol limit sensible or indeed legal for driving, I had to get on my own moped and follow the police to the station. After weaving in and out of traffic, stopping at lights, bleary and tired from hours of running around and filled with more than my fair share of noxious, heady substances, I eventually arrived.

* * * *

'How long have you been in here?'

'Four months.'

'Just in this room?' I said. 'What for?'

'They found me with pills,' replied the French guy, with a shrug. 'My girlfriend told them.'

I had just finished reading a book about how ex-pats get holed away in Thai prisons for years, forgotten about, falsely accused. And now this guy was confirming my worst suspicions.

After my scary twenty-minute ride across the island, I had been led to this room. I had barely been able to see the walls in the dark, but I could tell by the way the sound resonated that it wasn't big. The door opening and closing revealed the details; it was no larger than a small living room, a few hammocks strung along the walls – dank, stifling and smelly. Stumbling in, I had been immediately overwhelmed by the sound of many voices shouting, screaming at me to remove my shoes; it's rude and uncouth in Thailand to remain shod indoors. In this case it was ironic, in a room where crawling, scurrying cockroaches shared the living space, and human waste overpowered the senses.

I'd made my way to a small corner, tucking my feet up, holding my knees, and trying not to give way to fear.

The door had opened again.

'George?' I had been pulled out and hauled before the chief commander within ten minutes. I was hoping, at best, that this was all somebody's idea of a sick joke.

'How is the football in England, George?'

'I'm not really sure.'

'Well, who do you support?'

'I don't really follow it.'

I was being grilled about the state of football in England, and my knowledge did not hold up. I really knew nothing about football, and I began to despair; maybe my future was dependent on having the right answers. I had none, and was soon back in the cell.

I'd crawled back into my corner. It was there I met the French guy. His story did nothing to allay my fears as I spent the night listening to the murmurs and snores of the Thai around me, desperately trying to mask my face, protecting myself from the stench coming from the hole in the floor; no privacy, no dignity for those in need of the toilet, and only a black bin of water to ease thirst, shared like a feeding trough. I tried not to spend the long, dark hours panicking. I never even thought about praying to the God who seemed so far away for help.

I was more fortunate than my French friend. The lawyer I had paid to look after our interests at the bar met me at the court the following day. I had to pay £500 in order to ensure my passport wasn't sent to Bangkok and I was expelled from the country; if that happened I'd lose the bar, everything. I paid £10 to the court, and the other £490 was divided up between all the Thai officials. But I recovered my freedom, fairly unscathed, save for my respect for Thai authority, and returned to work, and to Saichon.

* * * *

I waved, squinting in the evening sunshine as Saichon was driven away in the back of a police van. Handcuffed, she gestured wildly, her face puce and obscenities pouring from her mouth.

We had rowed. I had locked the door to the bar, shutting her out. Saichon, fuelled by drink, had picked up a beer bottle and thrown it through the door, sending millions of fragments of glass shooting everywhere. The police were called.

The novelty had been wearing off for some time now. It was like when you buy a pair of new shoes; the excitement of newness soon fades when the scuff marks appear.

In truth, everything around me had begun to scuff and fade. Sam had a nasty accident on his moped not long after we bought the bar; maybe he took the corner too quickly, or perhaps it was the result of too much alcohol and not enough sleep. Anyway, he decided to head back to England; scars and tattered skin had removed all the magic for him. My friendship with Greg was tense and troubled by the relationship with Saichon; she was a handful when she was drunk, and our fighting was frequent. In moments of passion we'd break up, screaming hate-filled obscenities at one another, only to get back together in the quieter, sober moments of tomorrow. But this evening was different. The shine had well and truly vanished.

As Saichon became a distant, shrieking spot on the horizon, depression started seeping into my soul. A repeated pattern, a downwards cycle, round and round, fighting, breaking up, making up. Along with the exhaustion of relationship strife, days at the bar were long and tiring, the evenings filled with drink and cocaine. Foreign lands had promised escape from Woking, what I had thought of as the problem; yet here I was, waving off my screaming girlfriend, to return to another night filled with the same old, same old.

Catching imaginary glimpses of Saichon with another man, and thinking about their night of passion, led me to the forged romance of a one-night stand. The careless flipping around in sheets as I tried to forget myself, us, was the final straw. I decided I wanted out.

Angry with paradise and all it hadn't delivered, I was disappointed with life. I had sought out in every nook and cranny for contentment and satisfaction, and had failed to find any lasting sense. We were also struggling to make ends meet. With another chap buying into the bar, and the idea of buying a shop to increase our income, I headed back to England. I was going to work to get enough money to buy a shop. I also needed to clear my head.

Chapter 11

Old Life, New Start

I pulled the heavy winter coat closer around my chest. It was still dark as I stumbled out of the house and down the street feeling chilly, sleepy and fed up. Beginning work at 6:30 a.m. in December in Britain was a harsh and cruel shock.

'George, what do you think you're doing? Load the turf this way. Stack them like this. You'll get more in.'

Darren, the guy we'd bought the bar from in Thailand, had become a harsh critic, finding it easy to rib, cajole and find fault. It had turned out that the simple act of pushing a wheelbarrow was a whole lot more complicated than I had believed. In fact, every role I had been given had turned into an opportunity for criticism. I wasn't up to scratch and I knew it, but I'd been keeping my hands clean and my body suntanned and relaxed, and the most physically demanding job I had done recently was pulling pints in Thailand. My life looked impossibly different, not just in geography.

'George, you idiot!' Darren laughed as the turf I'd piled high, in the way he suggested, tumbled to the ground. I would pay for this, but Darren loved it. The business was his – landscape gardening – and the accommodation we stayed in was his, too; a three-bedroom house in Romford, Essex. He had access to all the power he wanted, and he loved to flaunt it.

Later that afternoon in the pub, I had to tell the story of my turf disaster.

'George, tell them about the turf, mate. Tell them, George.'

Darren announced the story to the whole pub, lapping up the attention, demanding stories were told that made him look good. Other times, he would ask me to tell everyone how big his house in Thailand had been, or he would boast himself about how beautiful his wife was, or get one of his brothers to admit that Darren's landscaping business was better than his. Darren had four brothers, each in business, and the competition was fierce. All the jibes about the turf just made me more determined to succeed; one day I managed to break all records by carrying twenty-eight rolls of turf in one wheelbarrow.

The days were backbreaking – early starts, no breaks, and with Darren always on my case, squeezing more from my muscles than I thought possible. But we'd finish around 4 p.m. and head to the pub, which was full of locals; the same faces, same routines, always there; we were known by name. I made friends with an old guy called Jeffrey. He'd smile a toothless grin, lighting up his face in a way that displayed his gentle manner – open, warm and easy; the sort of gentleness that is abused. He'd been hurt, walked over. He just got by, drinking his nights away, spending time with the fruit machine and any other locals who would give him the time of day. Sometimes, to break up the monotony, he would come and work for Darren.

'Got any of the white stuff, mate?'

I'd lined up my bar stool next to one of the known drug dealers in the area, a regular at the pub. Agreements, exchanges, offers frequently tossed back and forth between punters and Alec in that pub, it was hardly covert operations. He leaned back against the bar, eyes fixated on the latest game of pool and the current winner who'd trumped everyone that evening, staying on for around ten games. Unbeatable. Alec's brow furrowed, either contemplating my request or the lack of games to be won on the pool table that night.

'Nah, I don't think so, mate.' Alec nodded towards Darren.

'Come on, Alec, my money's good. He won't find out.'

'Not tonight, George. Maybe another time.'

I knew what that meant – when Darren wasn't there . . . or never. Working for Darren, living in his house, had cast some kind of drug-free zone over me. Darren and his family were well known in the area, and brought with them a certain amount of fear and respect; drugs were a no-no to them, and so those associated with them would not be considered safe to supply. I would occasionally get a line of coke or two, that was all. It was frustrating.

And so entertainment had to be of the cheap and repet-itive kind. Alongside the fruit machines, hours would be whiled away on the pool tables. Pints would be downed, but I'd rarely pay. The reward for putting up with Darren was that he'd always see that we were looked after; that was the deal. At the end of the working day, £60 cash in hand, having had a few beers and being given a roof over our heads, we'd tumble back home at 11 p.m. where Darren's Thai wife would have dinner on the table for us. She was beautiful, as Darren would boast, but she must have been lonely.

'George, this is my brother, Craig.'

'All right, George?'

I was somewhat taken aback by the high-pitched voice. I shook Craig's outstretched hand. 'All right, mate?'

'Craig's gonna stay with us for a bit,' said Darren.

I wondered exactly where. We were already crammed into a three-bedroom house in an area full of 'wide-boys' going nowhere fast but believing, or rather hoping, they were 'someone'. The place was pretty crowded; it already housed Darren's family, Hugo – a Belgian guy that we had met in Thailand – and me. I occupied a converted loft room, with an outdated TV for company. Hugo had a Thai wife and son living with him – all three of them in one room. The only place left for Craig to sleep was on the sofa. Craig had not long left prison. He had disdain for his brother, and a heroin problem. But he was family and there was always work that needed doing.

'Craig, George, can you start putting that fence up?'

I surveyed the ground, the tools and my working companion. The fencing job was massive and would take a lot of work. Feet-deep holes would need to be dug for every concrete post before anything else could go up.

'Right, let's get started.' Craig's rather squeaky voice grated on me, and I nodded grimly. By about lunchtime I realized that I was far behind Craig's work pace. I stood, rubbing my aching back for a second while I watched him. Craig was digging a hole no deeper than a few inches, just enough for the post to be able to stand up for a couple of days. Craig glanced up, and saw me looking over.

'I'm off, George. Pretty much done anyway.'

Brushing his hands nonchalantly on his clothes, he lay down his tools and walked away, most likely off for a fix, while I was left to redo all his work. I returned to the house that evening, sweaty and frustrated. I banged around in the bathroom as I turned on the shower taps, hoping the heat and steam would calm me down.

The clothes I'd discarded the night before lay strewn across my bedroom floor, a few coins scattered here and there, having spun from my pockets. I picked them up to put in the pint glass that sat on my shelf. It was for pound coins. But it had gone.

'*Craig!*' I was livid. I wasn't sure he could annoy me any more than he already had. But being the only one in the house, along with his son who had come to visit, there was no other culprit. And it wasn't the first time.

'What's up, mate?'

'What've you done with my pint glass?'

'Dunno what you're talking about.'

'It was here before I took my shower and now it's gone. Give it back. It's not funny.' Energy began to drain from me. I wanted to shout, but I just couldn't be bothered.

He blamed his 11-year-old son. 'He was here too, George.' He began to go on about what he would do when he got his hands on the little thief. I wasn't convinced.

A week later Craig owned up, but I was getting tired of it all; the cramped house and the endless monotony of a life dominated by hard work and nights spent in the pub. I wanted to stay away from the drinking, but had nothing to do otherwise. An empty, futile existence; aimless and ambling, I felt as if I was going nowhere.

There was a church I'd walk past on my way to and from the pub. The posters on the billboards promised new life, a hope and future, if I turned to Jesus. One day, I stopped. It reminded me of so many things I'd believed in but never carried on with. For a moment, it gripped my heart. But I shrugged off the feelings – yes, I believed in God, but . . . Anyway, I walked on.

* * * *

'Right, let's go see how Hugo has been getting on.' It was mid-afternoon; the worst of winter was over but the evenings were still in a hurry to drag the light away from the day. This always made working arduous; lots to be done before we could no longer see where to dig, carry or drop.

'Hugo had better got most of that turfing sorted.'

Left for the day with a massive job, it was typical for Darren to expect a lot in a short amount of time. The garden had been around the size of five tennis courts and Hugo had to take the top layer of turf off, getting as much done as he could before we arrived to help.

'What the . . . ?' As we swung into the drive of the house, we saw Hugo sat in the wheelbarrow, legs dangling, smoking. Nearby, the radio hummed lazily, keeping him company in his afternoon of leisure. Darren jumped from the van, mirrored by Hugo's own hasty ascent. Casting my eyes round the garden, I could see Hugo had done the tiniest patch and definitely not a full day's work.

'Hugo! What do you think you're playing at?' In broken English and confused tones, throwing his arms around just like Manuel from *Fawlty Towers*, Hugo concocted his explanation.

'The council. The men, they came. They told me I could not leave the grass on the pavement. I did not know what to do. I do not understand the English. The stupid English!'

'Why didn't you call?'

'My battery, it was dead. I try. I so angry!' Taken in by Hugo's dramatic expression of anger, and his lack of English, Darren let it go, and Hugo got away with a day off.

Hugo never failed to amuse me. But a couple of weeks later, he'd had enough. He and I were digging footings in Darren's garden for his new extension. I considered, at that moment, that we were Darren's little slaves.

The fine rain was falling almost horizontally, blown by a brisk wind; winter's final onslaught before it was chased off by spring. I could barely feel my fingers, and I shivered as my feet slipped around in the trench that we'd dug. With a few inches of water sloshing around at our feet, my toes were chafing with the combination of wet, soaked socks and skin. Hugo was a few feet ahead of me in the trench, head bowed.

'All right, Hugo?'

He grunted.

'Let's just do a bit more and then get a cup of tea.'

Still nothing more than a grunt.

I carried on, chipping away at the earth with my spade, just as I saw Hugo climb out of the trench. He stood up and lobbed his spade, mud and all, across the road, landing a few feet from a neighbour's car.

'Hugo? You all right, mate?'

He said nothing, opened the front door of the house, and went inside. I carried on digging. Ten minutes later, Hugo reappeared, wearing clean clothes. He walked down the path, turned right along the street, and I never saw him again. It turned out, having told no one, he had already bought tickets for Thailand. He left that day.

A few months later I, too, left, leaving only a note for Darren on my departure. I'd had enough. I was fed up with waiting for Greg to return to help produce income for the shop. There was always an excuse; a problem with the girlfriend, a problem with the girlfriend's mum, more reasons stacking higher, leaving me with only one desire – to be out of it. Eventually Greg did return, but all my enthusiasm had vanished. Thailand seemed a distant memory, hot and humid with the temperature of failed promises and broken relationships, and I just couldn't be bothered with it any more. Knowing my problems weren't going to be solved in Thailand, I was ready to move on, and we sold the bar.

* * * *

Another fresh start, a clean slate to write on. This time I would be happy, I decided, as I stepped off the plane. I could be myself. The bar had gone, the backbreaking work, the disempowerment of life with Darren. I was free to start again.

'Hiya, Mum.'

'It's good to see you, George.' Mum threw her arms round me, and I kissed her on the cheek. Meeting Mum in an airport like this was new, unusual. Mum had disconnected herself from everything she had previously known. No longer bound by familiar memories, the old house in Woking, Dad and domestic duties, she seemed different, larger, a person in her own right and not just a mother. She drove me home to her new villa and her new husband, Roy.

In England, September had been bringing with it the promise of winter; cooler mornings hinted at frost to come. Leaves, beginning to surrender their green vibrancy to flaming hues, were soon to be ripped away and flung down to create carpets of fire by aggressive winds. The summer holidays had ended and children had reluctantly returned to school.

For me, at 26, it felt as if the holiday was just beginning as I gazed over Paphos from my bedroom window. The sea glistened and danced as Cyprus continued to enjoy warm temperatures and humid highs. I could see the town rising in a tide of white-washed houses, juxtaposed with lush greenery and the red slate of churches. I was excited to discover what Cyprus had for me, and determined this time that things would be good.

It was my English accent that probably got me the job. I would hop on my hired moped and spin through the mountains for an hour every day just to sell cigarettes over the phone to Americans, and then resolve the problem of customs when they were seized on dispatch. The company was poorly run, and I began to feel the familiar drain of boredom and monotony. Still, the ride on the moped lifted my spirits each day – mountains reaching into the sky and dropping away to the sea, cloudless days where the sun hit corners of the mountains in angles of orange delight. At points I would be so high in the mountains that, despite the heat of the evening sun, I would shiver in the chilly air. But the travelling was tiring and expensive, and I bought myself a flat on the other side of the island from Mum and Roy, to be nearer work. And so began my loneliest days.

It was like staring into a hole of nothingness. Once again I had everything; a job, a moped, a flat that had its own swimming pool, a beautiful country to live in. But there was always something missing, and this time it was people. I knew no one, had no connections, and would return to my flat each evening to lose myself in a void of beer, food and porn.

As a teenager, food was an addiction, something that temporarily filled a gap. A chocolate bar would lift my spirits as I removed the wrapper, stuffed it into my mouth, felt the surge of sugar course through my veins and my endorphins nod with agreement. And then it would be over. It was the same with porn; I watched, I viewed, I sought to climb into the screen with those people, to be part of something, to feel something, to not be quite so alone. The high, the release, was fleeting, and I was never satiated.

There were times, late into the night, when a joint would be passed around at work. The familiar sight and smell drew me back into the good times I could remember – the highs, the giggles, just like before, yet with adult ferocity and need. It didn't matter how I tried to fill the hunger, or quieten the grumbles and murmurs of appetite, the question refused to be suppressed. Cyprus began to lose its appeal and I longed for home. It wasn't long before I was back in familiar territory.

Nothing changed as I settled back into life in Woking. Living with an old school friend, I quickly became absorbed in the old routine. Work filled my days, and alcohol and cocaine, my nights. I was acutely aware of being trapped, wanting to say no, urging my mind to be controlled, disciplined; every night I found myself giving in. I knew I could do whatever I wanted, but freedom was a complete illusion as I was bound to drink, drugs and selfishness.

Chapter 12

The Lost Son

I looked at the sign rammed in the ground, always filled with posters, cheesy catchphrases promising new life, inviting the outsider in. It was a church I walked by every night after a few beers at my mate's. A familiar route, a familiar church, a familiar poster-board. However, it wasn't the first time I'd felt a tugging, nudging. I would keep on walking, promising myself that some day I'd step inside, look back into the religion I'd dabbled with in my teens.

Then one Saturday, I was convicted inside: 'Do it tomorrow. Go to church. Set your alarm. Get up. Get it over with.' As soon as I got home that night, I set my alarm.

'There are no half measures with Jesus,' the vicar said as I shifted in my seat, surrounded by a circle of twenty old ladies. 'Jesus wants everything. You have to commit everything you have.' The idea disturbed my sense of everything being OK because I believed in God. Surely that was enough, wasn't it? According to this vicar, it wasn't, and it made me feel uneasy, unsure, vulnerable. I filled out a card expressing my desire to know more. Later, a lady met me at my flat. She brought a pile of books and an invitation to a church weekend away.

*   *   *   *

'Hiya, chum!' Puppy-dog eagerness overtook me as Steve threw his arms around me.

'Long time no see.' It had been twelve years since I'd been to St John's. Nothing much had changed. Greying hair, deepened lines on faces, newborns and new faces. I slipped into familiar territory with everything within me feeling unfamiliar, clunky, afraid.

'Open your Bibles at Luke chapter 15 verse 11 and we'll read together.'

Reading, explaining, exposing. A hush enveloped my heart and my ears hung on every word.

As I listened, I understood that in Luke 15, the story of the lost son, Jesus is speaking to two very different groups of people – those who think they are good enough for God, and the social outcasts. He tells them of a family where a man had two sons. The younger son wants his inheritance, even though his father hasn't yet died. He takes the money, leaving to make friends and party hard. Extreme partying leads to a broken bank, a broken man. All that is left is a job feeding slops to pigs, with the boy so hungry that his mouth waters at the sight of their luxury. At the end of himself, skin hanging from visible bones, depression consuming his being, he knows his only hope is to return to his dad. He'll beg for forgiveness, beg to be a slave. But his father, watching and waiting for this day, runs to meet him, taking him up in his arms, and the thought of slavery is cast aside. Sonship resumed, a party is thrown, a totally undeserved and extravagant expression of love.

'So you see, we're all like this son. We have turned our back on our heavenly Father, preferring to do whatever we want.

God, like the father in the story, wants us back.' The preacher started to conclude his sermon. 'We can run to him, return to him, despite everything we have done, and know that he forgives us and welcomes us. Have you done that? Will you do that?'

At the first notes from the piano in the corner, I stood to sing, tears streaming down my face. I knew that was me. I was the son who had run away from my heavenly Father – God. Spending money, taking drugs, sleeping with women were merely symptoms of a deadly disease. My heart had abandoned God. I'd never given everything to him; I'd kept myself back. But here was a welcome, acceptance, forgiveness, as though God was right next to me, whispering to my sad, withered-up heart: 'I know what you've done. You know what you've done. But you can come back. It's OK. You don't need to perform.'

It is hard for me to explain the magnitude of the situation I found myself in; it was as if the whole of my life had been coming to this point. More than destiny, so much more than fate, this was like the meeting of two worlds – my old, pointless world, and a new, exciting world.

All those years I had felt something was missing; it was the feeling you get when, off on holiday, you think you have forgotten or lost something. You're going through everything you've packed to try to figure out what it is that's missing.

With the tears, the pent-up sadness was released. Where pain had shrivelled my heart, turning it into a thing of ugliness, what I was experiencing now was pure, better than any drug, any girl, any job, anything. I felt stripped away, scraped out and given something new of value, of purity, freedom. The thing I had been searching for all my life had finally found me. That feeling of not quite knowing what I had been looking for was gone in those few minutes; there had been years of scrambling, and yet all was sorted out in moments. The search was over. The feelings I'd been experiencing became labelled, understood, contextualized – lost, although I only knew I was lost the moment I felt found. I wanted to tell God how sorry I was, how I wanted to know him, how I wanted to come home. And I understood I could, because Jesus had taken the punishment I'd deserved when he died on the cross. He rose from the dead so I could live a new, clean life. I cried, sorrow being replaced with the relief of knowing truth, mercy, forgiveness. I had experienced strange spirits in my time, but from that moment on, God himself came to live in me; the Holy Spirit was inside me, helping me to live this new life in his power, not my own.

* * * *

'George, I haven't heard from Dad.'

Sometimes my sister wouldn't hear from Dad for a few days – too many days for everything to be OK. I would go round, bracing myself for what I would find; piles of letters behind the door, stacks of cans, human excrement and Dad passed out in an alcoholic stupor on his chair, or the floor. But he would always be all right.

'Have you tried calling?' I asked.

'I left a message,' she said, 'but he hasn't called back.'

'OK. I'll go round.'

Massive changes had begun to occur since the day I'd understood about the lost son. I'd wanted change; I had looked for it all those years, but this was different. It was lasting and real and not driven by a desire to get more, feel more, be more. There were questions, doubts, uncertainties, but I read carefully and asked questions until I was satisfied with the answers. And the drinking, the smoking, they stopped as my desires, ambitions and heart changed. God was doing it.

My relationship with Dad always had this dark shadow cast across it; it was a relationship marred by alcohol, and I carried around a deep sense of anger that he loved his drink more than he loved me. As I started to grow in my relationship with God, I began to understand that just as God had forgiven me, I had to forgive my dad. One night, through floods of tears, I gave up hating my dad and asked God to take away my anger, my bitterness, my desire for revenge. I wept like I've never wept before as I began to understand his pain and hurt. I knew Dad had become a slave to his freedom, a freedom which led to bondage, to chains to a bottle. Like a dog on a leash, alcohol was never far from his sight. Understanding this led me to see things differently.

'Dad says you're a fanatic, George.' My sister had filled me in on Dad's opinion of me. When she'd told me this, I'd just been round to see him and been able to tell him of God's love for him and pray for him.

I reflected on this as I knocked on Dad's door a few months later. I shouted through the letter box. There was no reply. Gingerly turning the spare key in the lock I prayed for the strength for what I might find.

Like colliding with a brick wall, the smell hit as soon as I stepped through the door. Cooped-up, gone off, dank and mostly indescribable, it was putrid. I turned down the hallway and looked left to the entrance of the lounge. Black, withered and motionless, a pair of legs poked out through the doorway. Everything within me churned twisted and sank. I fled.

'God, you're going to have to take over, I can't do this. God, I can't do this.' Over and over I repeated until the thought struck me that maybe he wasn't dead, maybe his legs were caught and he couldn't move. I turned the car round and drove back. A journey of minutes seeming like a lifetime.

I will never forget the look on my Dad's face as I stared down at his decaying body, lying on the floor that day in 2009. The look of life sucked away; fear, misery, death itself. His lips had receded so his teeth were visible, and his fingers had shrivelled, pointy and long like the branches of an old tree. And the maggots; maggots moved and squirmed from every orifice.

I found out then that God doesn't shield us from difficult things, from suffering, but he does walk through it with us. I can honestly say I was never angry with God about my dad. God could have saved him; he could have intervened in different ways. But as I looked to Jesus on the cross, it gave me fresh insight into how God must have felt to watch his Son die in agonizing pain. If he loved me enough to inflict the judgement I deserved on his Son instead of on me, I could trust him through this trial. And that renewed my strength.

I have had so many questions, and I still do, but one by one, I am finding answers. The thing I have been searching for, that missing piece – meaning, purpose and assurance – has found me. His name is Jesus. Right from the first moment I entered into a real relationship with the God of the universe, my heart began a process of change and transformation.

*   *   *   *

'Rainbow Towers' was mid-party the night I realized I liked Kate. Our friends nicknamed our house this; there were three men living together like George, Zippy and Bungle from the children's show. But I was exhausted and not much in the mood to talk to all the people filling our spaces, eating, drinking, having a good time. Kate, a friend from church, sat opposite me at the kitchen table, chatting. An hour passed by easily, contentedly. Making her excuses, she moved to the other room.

As my eyes followed, I was annoyed, upset, dejected. Demanding my inner dialogue account for itself, I debated the meaning of this emotion as I got up and followed her. An hour or so later, she left the party. I was gutted.

Texting her the following day, I asked if the jumper left behind on our sofa was hers – knowing full well it wasn't. Four hours and 400 texts later, I asked her, like a 13-year-old, 'Do you like me?' She did, and we became 'an item'.

When my father died, he left me some money, which I used five months later to fly Kate and me to Paris.

Journeying there I thanked God that something beautiful could come from the ashes of death; not just the money, but the gift of a new, healthy relationship. In front of the Eiffel Tower, I got down on one knee and asked Kate to be my bride. I felt so vulnerable waiting for her answer, holding her gaze, heart pounding. I think Jesus does the same for us; invites us into a lifelong relationship with him; we only have to accept. In the shadow of France's most famous landmark, Kate said yes. But the road still isn't easy. It wasn't easy the day I asked Kate to marry me, it wasn't in the years prior to meeting her, and it isn't today. Mistakes are still made.

God tells us that he is able to do more than we ask or even imagine. I see a small glimpse of this in my relationship with Kate. But where my other relationships led to emptiness, now I have Christ at the centre; it means I don't need to 'use' Kate to become happy. The void is filled; I am free to love her. I never felt safe in relationships, worried the other person would run when the real George was exposed; that the darkness of reality would eclipse anything good. Keeping my guard up, the pressure of need would crush me. And I was selfish. With Kate, it is all so totally different in every way. I love her and delight in her. And where once my relationships were dominated by the desire for sex, we grew close as we understood each other and our relationship with God. And now, our marriage is a great reflection of the type of relationship Jesus has with his people: totally committed and totally faithful. Through disagreements, there is no fear.

*   *   *   *

Early on in my Christian life, before I met Kate, I made a big mistake. Three months after that moment of clarity in church, where the story of the lost son hit me so profoundly, I found myself working in a care home, earning money, putting my life back together. I was high; high on all I had been experiencing and learning about God and, ironically, filled with arrogance. Somewhere between understanding that God had done it all for me, and that I was incapable of living in the way God wanted me to, in my own strength. I forgot that it was all down to God, and that I needed him.

She was attractive, friendly, and engaged to someone else. And yet I slept with her.

I woke up the next morning, broken, in bits, feeling as if my relationship with God was over. How could I go on now? How could I call myself a Christian? How could I ask God for forgiveness? I had paraded my change in front of my friends, shouting of my newfound love for Jesus. But now I felt I had made a mess of everything. It seemed I had not changed at all.

Eaten up inside, I continued in the relationship. I stopped going to church and drifted into a feeling of no-man's land. I still believed, but I could not face who I was. Then a friend shared of how the mistakes he had made cost someone their life, he spent time in prison. But there was no question for him of God's love, forgiveness, acceptance. I began to wonder whether God might still be able to take me back. Through prayer, a good friend, and stumbling back into church one Sunday, I discovered God was still there; I needed to go back, stop what I was doing, and believe that there is nothing that adds or takes away from God's love; Jesus' death was and is enough to forgive everything that I have done or will do. God does it all, and my mistakes cannot alter that forgiveness, love, grace.

Looking back, I see the battle, the one I fought – or rather was fought for me – on the railway tracks; the spiritual. The battle we don't see with our physical eyes, but is there. Just as demons masquerading as good spirits of dead people tried to destroy me, I believe God somehow rescued me from the train. It is a battle I still fight as I continue to want to follow God, and so many other things scream for attention, love, worship. I used to struggle with that thought; I used to think we should only believe in what we can see. But someone pointed out to me that I cannot see the wind, I cannot see my mum's love for me, I cannot see a text message that is floating around in the air, but they are there. The same is true for God. He is all around us, if only we will look, willing to lift us out of darkness and give us life and hope.

Epilogue

Apparently, in Greek, my name means Peasant Farmer. When asked, I would say instead that it meant 'King'. Something grander, more fitting for who I thought I was. Recently, walking through a field, the ground ploughed up, I sensed that God might be readdressing my pride, replacing my own ideas with his words of truth. He was telling me things I could do to serve him, and that I must make him the rightful King of my life. Like the farmer will sow seeds in that field to bring about a crop of wheat or barley, so I believe God has called me to use words like seeds, telling others about him.

What can so change a man like me – a man who'd been into the reality of the occult, into drugs and casual sex and a selfish, futile way of living – that he gives up everything to follow Jesus? What can so change someone that they find peace and purpose that can't be found anywhere else? I tried just about everything to find meaning, as you have read in my story. But ultimately, nothing brought lasting satisfaction.

Today I work with an organization called Lumina Ministries speaking in churches, schools, prisons and universities, sharing the amazing news of Jesus Christ, and teaching and training others to do the same. I have seen God working miracles in people's lives, from those in the worst prisons to some of the richest businessmen in the world. I don't get a salary for the work I do, God supplies in many ways; what Jesus has done for me has given me a burning passion to tell others about him. God can and does transform lives.

I am still based in Woking, Surrey, with my wife, Kate, trying to tell as many people as I can about this amazing God who loves us and wants to rescue us from the mess we often make of our lives.

I am hoping my story may have resonated with you in some way; whoever you are, whatever you've done, you can know God because of Jesus' death on the cross for all your wrong thoughts and actions. Perhaps you feel bound by your past, or your present; maybe you are even experiencing things very similar to what I have described. You can call out to God now; ask him to reveal himself to you, as well as the dark places of your heart and life. He can forgive and change anything. Or maybe you would like further information about becoming free of the occult, drugs or a broken sexuality. There are plenty of people able to support and help. I would love to hear from you and talk to you about *your* journey.

Contact me at george@luminaministries.com. The Lighthouse, 8–10 High Street, Woking, Surrey, GU21 6BG.

We are also able to supply you with details of local evangelical churches that will be able to talk with you.

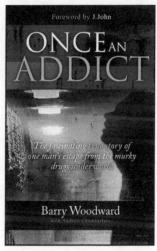

Once an Addict

The Fascinating True Story of One Man's Escape from the Murky Drugs Underworld

Barry Woodward
with Andrew Chamberlain

Barry Woodward was a drug dealer and heroin addict who once lived on the notorious Bull Rings in the centre of Manchester. *Once an Addict* describes Barry's descent into the murky underworld of drug dealing, addiction, crime and imprisonment. Along the way we are introduced to some of the most extraordinary characters, and we see the extreme lengths to which some of them will go to get their next 'fix'. Illegal drug use claimed the lives of many such people, and it seemed inevitable that Barry would also succumb to the consequences of his addiction.

With devastating amphetamine-induced mental health issues, a fourteen-year heroin addiction, a string of broken relationships, and the threat of HIV looming, the outlook for Barry appeared very bleak. Then three extraordinary encounters changed his life forever . . .

978-1-86024-602-9

Tough Talk 2

*More Life-Changing
Stories from the
Tough Talk Team*

with Millie Murray

Joe Lampshire – '"YOU WILL DIE" . . . Playing the Ouija board was just for a laugh; I had done it many times before. But this was something way, way out of my experience and it wasn't funny.' For Joe, this was just the beginning of a long battle with the spirit world. As dark forces threatened to claim Joe's life, could light ever break through?

Martyn Parrish – 'It was heady stuff and, of course, I wanted to do it again. I wanted to drop some pills and then ride my bike. This was living! Or so I thought.' At first the drugs freed Martyn's mind, and then they began to completely take over. As heroin became Martyn's closest and most destructive friend, could he ever find peace?

Simon Pinchbeck – 'I'd been greedy, thinking how much I'd make out of my investment, and now it was gone. I felt the need to settle the matter, preferably by slowly killing each man involved.' A hunger for money and involvement with tough and violent police corps had sent Simon's life spiralling out of control. Deserted by friends and in huge debt, would he ever find a way out?

978-1-86024-700-2

The Power &
the Glory

The Remarkable Story of
a Four-Time World
Powerlifting Champion

Arthur White and
Martin Saunders

Arthur White had it all. Not only was he a successful businessman and happy family man, but as a champion powerlifter, he was literally on top of the world. But when he got to the top, he wasn't satisfied . . .

As he searched for a greater high, Arthur's life spiralled out of control. Drug addiction, an intense affair and a descent into violence followed, and before long death seemed like the only way out. As he stared into the abyss, an incredible encounter turned Arthur's life upside down. He would never be the same again . . .

978-1-86024-560-2

**Conquering
the
Dragon**

Kim Goh

'I put the gun to my head, closed my eyes and I pulled the trigger.' For Kim Goh, caught up in a tangle of gang culture and drugs, this was just one of many life-threatening situations.

A successful businessman by the age of eighteen, Kim Goh's violent pursuits and ability to con people kept him from settling in countries for long. From Thailand to Minorca, New York to Switzerland, his life became more chaotic and restless as he indulged in gambling, drugs, alcohol and sex. Climbing his way up the career ladder of a UK triad, Kim soon found that his volatile nature caused his behaviour to spiral out of control with devastating consequences.

A gripping tale of a man searching for meaning and of a God whose intervention is both dramatic and life changing.

978-1-86024-616-6

Authentic

We trust you enjoyed reading this book
from Authentic Media. If you want to be
informed of any new titles from this author
and other exciting releases you can sign up
to the Authentic newsletter online:

www.authenticmedia.co.uk

Contact us:

By post:
Authentic Media
52 Presley Way
Crownhill
Milton Keynes
MK8 0ES

E-mail:
info@authenticmedia.co.uk

Follow us: